LISTEN TO WHAT PEOPLE ARE SAYING ABOUT
LEARNING TO BE HUMAN AGAIN
BY MATT LANDRY

"The book is full of insight, and a unique wisdom blended with occasional humor the author masterfully articulates his message to the reader audience. I would certainly like to see this made into a series because it is full of themes that we can all relate to in order to live as greater human beings."
~Scott Allan - Author of *Rejection Proof*, *Empower Your Life*, and *Do It Scared*

"It's a wonderfully insightful guide to the inner workings of the human condition. Highly articulate and written from the standpoint of someone who truly cares about and empathizes with his fellow man."
~James LaPierre

"I've read a lot of "personal development" type books over the last 5+ years, but what I love about this book is that Matt provides simple, yet specific steps you can take to easily APPLY the insights he shares. And if you do, I guarantee they will have a profound impact on your life."
~Stefano Ganddini - Millennial Success Coach

Learning to Be Human Again

Do You Remember Who You Were

Before the World Told You Who You Should Be?

Matt Landry

Copyright 2017 all rights reserved

My gift to you.

As a thank you for purchasing or reading *Learning to Be Human Again*, I'd love to give you a ***free*** eBook.

We could all use a little extra confidence and some assistance with our self-worth. I've compiled a simple guide that contains 20 easy ways to help you do it!

Just use the web address below to get your copy today!

http://www.mattlandry.com/free_confidence_book

I am grateful for both your support and time. I sincerely hope you enjoy it.

Learning to Be Human Again

Contents

1. *Introduction*

2. *Learning to be Human Again*

3. *Who Am I? What You Are, and What You are Not*

4. *Victims of Programming and Creatures of Habit*

5. *Ego - Am I Winning? Who's keeping Score?*

6. *False Expectations*

7. *Emotions*

8. *Our Want for Comfort, the Value in Feeling Uncomfortable*

9. *Embracing Mistakes, Encouraging Failures*

10. *Priorities and Values*

11. *Can't We All Just Get Along? (Communication)*

12. *Compassion, Empathy, and Forgiveness*

13. *Conclusion*

Introduction

I believe that at the heart of us all lies an unspoken feeling we perceive but have buried deep within ourselves. We know that in our busy lives, there has to be something more, yet, at the same time, so much less. We all long for a simplicity that we seem to have an inkling of but just can't put our finger on. We want to know who we were before everyone told us who we should be, how we can be more authentic with ourselves, and give some necessary attention to who we think we were genuinely created to be. We want a meaningful life without all the pressures inherent in what society wants us to feel, see, believe, and think.

We've never been as depressed, anxious, or stressed as we are today. Learning to strip away the unnecessary pressures and societal expectations we've either placed upon ourselves or have had dumped on us, and living simply as a human animal would be undeniably beneficial for our own sanity and that of everyone around us.

One of the goals of this book is to help reveal who we are as humans, deep down inside, minus the clutter and the noise of our brain, society, the media, technology, and the unnecessary need to somehow feel superior to our fellow humans.

This book, simply put, is an attempt to help flush out who you really are, not what you think everyone else assumes you should be. In these writings, I'll provide some insight and tools to separate the real you from the you who gets presented to the public, the you who experiences too much stress, fear, pain, suffering, shame, and guilt. These emotions are necessary to help guide us and get along with our fellow humans more effectively. However, we tend to exacerbate these feelings to imprison our true selves, fearful of what people might think if we don't conform or give them what we perceive they want to see.

Much of these writings are based upon my own journey, assembled from the journaling that helped me make sense of my own life. Reflecting upon my past experiences, I've assembled a collection of thoughts and solutions. It's going to contain some proven methods for uncovering your humanness, sprinkled with some personal opinion and philosophy. Some you may agree with, some you may not. Either way, my wish is that this book challenges you in some way to grow and learn.

I'm not a doctor or psychiatrist; I'm an observer and thinker. I've worked with the general public or managed people in one form or another for over thirty years, and from a young age, always looked at the world a little differently. I've tried to make sense of why people (including myself) do the things we do, either as individuals or in groups.

The actions of humans and society have always baffled me. Like everyone else, I've tried to fit in, have done some foolish things, made unnecessary mistakes, and have been through major depression twice. I've seen many highs and lows.

You may already know much of the information and be familiar with many of the concepts in this book, but that's perfectly acceptable. A reaffirmation of knowledge can be a comforting reminder. You may know more concepts in this book than you think but never saw them written down, or presented the way I'll present them to you. My purpose in creating this book is to help you think. If I can assist you in pulling a few tools or thoughts out of these chapters that will guide you to grow in some positive way, I will have succeeded.

I'm going to ask a few things as we go along, so keep a notebook handy to answer several questions and perform some exercises. I won't ask you to fill out a lot of information. I will, however, ask you to think about quite a bit. Take it in small chunks, and digest what you're reading.

I ask that you read the book from front to back your first time around. Certain sections may be helpful to refer back to later, but I've written this in such a manner that each chapter builds upon itself to the next.

So enjoy. These pages were a labor of love for me, and I hope I can, in some way, help you along on your personal journey.

Learning to Be Human Again

We've been preprogrammed at birth with an instinctual hardwiring for some of our feelings and actions. As we grew, we received additional, outside programming from the media, society, our parents, peers, and religion about the way we should look and act. The good news is that most of these programmings can be reversed if we choose, and we can start habitually thinking a new way. We can learn to become who we really are, instead of what we've been told we should be.

First, in trying to better understand the preprogramming we were born with, let's not forget that we're animals. By that, I mean mammals, just like a mouse, a monkey, or a moose. We're flesh and blood that needs to eat, drink, and breathe to survive. Just like many other animals, we were born with instinctual knowledge in order to survive. How does a mother bird know how long to sit on a nest of eggs to hatch them? How does she even know to sit on them to begin with? These weren't taught actions; they were already there when that bird was born. In many ways, we're no different. We have many preprogrammed instincts.

Self-preservation, or the fight or flight response, is one those preprogrammed instincts hardwired into our brain. Nature endowed us with this to ensure the proliferation and continuation of the human race. Without it, humans could have very well become extinct a long, long time ago.

Thousands of years past, the need for this instinct literally meant life or death. The human race was often plagued by starvation, illness, and attack from other tribes or wild animals. This built-in need for endurance and longevity provided early humans with the mental sharpness and tools to either outrun or outfight their predators, serve each other well in a community (as a matter of life or death), and gather food to ward off starvation. This survival instinct had a genuine place in our development, ensuring that the strongest, smartest, and most attractive humans would carry on the existence of the human race.

As we evolved as a species, that need for literal self-preservation slowly disappeared. Food was more abundant, and wild animal attacks diminished. The instinct was still there, but we morphed the conditions to which we applied them. This modern version of survival of the fittest has less to do with impressing the opposite sex with our brute strength, fighting off wild beasts, or skills in providing food. It has more to do with how much we own, how well we look, how much we earn, and other absurd notions we've devised to outdo one another in the struggle for status, which has replaced the need for survival. Tools that ensured safety and staying alive made sense but are no longer necessary. New rules have changed the face of survival for most, but we never learned to adapt to play the game of life differently. We're still hardwired to belong to a group and compete for our very existence. We still think we need to assert our egos for the sake of physical survival. In many ways, we're now fighting more for our emotional survival, which, in some cases, is more difficult to navigate than the physical realm.

To summarize, as part of our instinctual nature, we developed a need to survive, and, in that need, we developed the need for sex, to attract a mate, belong to a tribe or community, and to make the decision to either fight or flee when things got serious. These notions held their important roles in keeping us safe, and, more importantly, keeping us alive! As time marched on, we weren't being chased by wild animals, physically challenged by our enemies, or foraging for our food anymore. Our instincts, however, remained, and they still rear their heads in self-perceived situations in which we feel threatened. That's why, for what seems like no real logical reason, we long to feel protected, safe, or loved and accepted.

As we go through the steps of unlearning both our preprogramming and programming, we'll discover that our behaviors and thoughts, even though some are hardwired in us, are all choices of free will that we can control at any time. If you haven't realized it already, we have the capability to change ourselves, our thinking and behaviors, at any time. Personally, I think that's a very refreshing notion

Please keep an open mind in going forward with this book. Sometimes, the unlearning process can be more difficult than the learning process itself. We'll be taking steps to peel back the layers of what you've learned to help discover who you really are, and what you really know to be true, not just what you've been told or taught. It can be discouraging, at first, to realize that we may have believed something our whole life that turned out to be untrue or simply fabricated by people who thought it was for our own benefit. But in the long run, we grow by leaps and bounds when we start taking the restraints others have imposed on us and start thinking for ourselves. It's freeing when we start thinking about our actions, especially our detrimental ones, and what we can do to rectify them.

I should also note here that many of the things we've been programmed with from the mentioned outside sources are actually true, and favorable to our overall safety and well-being. Most are instrumental and beneficial in our growth and structured lives. What I'm asking in the coming pages isn't to throw away everything you know, or believe. I'm just asking you put some of it to your personal belief tests to make sure they still hold water. I'm asking you to ask yourself if you still believe them to be in fact, true to you.

When you stop to think about it, whether consciously, unconsciously, actively, or passively, we've really created ourselves. With others' help, obviously. But we're right where we are, because we ultimately chose it. Many may argue that's not the case, but it's true. The good news is that we can create ourselves to be something else. With the willingness to see things objectively, that's a very possible goal. You'll find that as we're able to change our perceptions about the way we think, we'll be able to change the stories associated with our lives. You'll soon discover that even with all of this programming, you're still the author of your life.

I used to think I was crazy for the way I thought. I would often scratch my head and ask, "Why on earth do people literally kill themselves trying to lose weight to look good and fit in? Why would someone use their power in such a horrible way to bully or belittle other people? Why do people think the size of their houses, cars, or bank accounts are an indication of their importance? Why would that make them somehow better or more valuable than me in this world?" None of these things made any logical sense (I realize now, that much of those have to do with the survival instinct we're born with, and the need for people to feel the need to display that in some form). Many of you may have thought the same things. As my journey has continued, I know more of you think that way than not. If you haven't thought of those things yet, then the following pages may help you to start.

We long to live out what our basic needs as a species calls to us to naturally be. We seem to have a basic, built-in knowledge that we're all good and created equal. We know that doing good for others is the right thing to do. We realize money is a wonderful tool for a successful life, but not an end in itself. Nurses and Doctors alike have long said that these kinds of things are often commonly realized at the end of life, which brings up an important point. What do you think people think about on their deathbeds? In hindsight, what was really important in their lives? Was it the house? Car? Was it all the time and energy spent on sports, music, or fashion? If you answered no, then you would be correct. Unfortunately, many of us find this out too late, and for some of us never at all.

What do you hope to accomplish before your life is over? I say this with good reason. I think that sometimes, as with many goals, I would suggest that you start with the end in mind, and recommend you come up with an end point to measure your success (or failure). To elaborate on that concept, an important exercise I think everyone should do at some point is to picture themselves at their own funeral. Stick with me here. We all go at some point, so we might as well realize that now and accept it. We aren't going to live forever. Nobody does, nobody has yet, anyway. Even if your beliefs take you to a better place after you die, there's no reason you can't make your life here on Earth an incredible and meaningful one.

Take a moment to think about this. Picture yourself as a visitor at your own funeral. Who would be there? What would they say about you? What were the things you would be proud of? Did you spend enough time with your family? Did you tell people you loved them? Did you confront people who needed to be confronted, in an adult, loving manner? Did you take the risks you should have? Did you live according to your values and principles? Were you kind and generous with your time and money?

EXERCISE:

Let's take the funeral concept one step further, and spend a few moments to write your own obituary. Go crazy here. You're in charge of it. Nobody is writing this one for you, it's all yours. What would it say? Again, would it be something that you would be proud of? Did you live a good life?

If you're having a difficult time thinking of what to say, and how to say it, visit the web address - http://www.remembranceprocess.com/capturing-a-life-in-words/guide-to-writing-an-obituary/ for a great guide on writing an obituary.

Go ahead and write your potential future obituary. Write your life story in a way that you would want it to go, not necessarily how it is right now at the moment. Take some serious time with this. The main point I'm making here is, do you want to live your life following the trends, an unhealthy or unnecessary need for success, or the constant need for some sort of needless approval?

When you finish, continue reading.

So how did you do? Did you write things like "She worried more than she needed to"? or "He never took the time to tell his children or friends he loved them"? or "She stressed out for so many years, she made herself physically sick"? Maybe, "She followed and tried to keep up with as many trends and expectations of her as possible" or "He spent every waking hour in front of his phone, ignoring all of those around him"? I hope not. That's the life too many of us are already living.

I assume your future obituary was hopeful, pleasant, and indicative of a life and time well spent. The good news is that however you wanted your life to be, you can start living that life now. After examining the life we hope to have lived, we can easily start creating it now, in the present.

To me, a life well lived, a successful one, is having been a devoted mother or father who not only provided for their families, but also spent the time to be with and teach their children. I view a life well spent as one that you continually improved by examining your belief structures and systems without being afraid of questioning the status quo and leading others in the same direction. A successful person is one who devoted their lives doing what they thought was right, not needing the acceptance of their peers, who took criticism well and ignored the petty judgments of others. He or she is someone who was generous and kind, willing to help others in need, and humble enough to accept their faults and not judge them for their choices. A person who has lived a good life is someone who ultimately was confident in who they were and was a beacon of encouragement and light to those around them.

This is my personal version of a life well lived. I hope you were willing and able to create your own definition of a what a good life is as well.

So join me, and let's relearn the reality of our basic needs before anyone told us what we should be or look like and before we adopted the ideas of society and tribal acceptances into our psyches.

Who Am I?
What You Are, and What You Are Not

Throughout much of this book, we'll address some labels that we put on ourselves that have been assigned to us by parents, peers, media, and religion; and that society deemed necessary to categorize us in. In dealing with, and removing a lot of these labels, you need to look at the most important label you identify yourself with and encounter.

Who am I?

When you look in the mirror, do you ever wonder who you are? Do you wonder who lives in that shell of bone and muscle? Humans have asked this question for a very, very long time. Humankind is the only species that has a sense of consciousness, which basically means that we're the only animals who can reason that we're actually alive.

So, let's try and answer that big picture question, who am I?

When presented with this challenge, most people would answer with their name. But I argue that your name is just another label. If your parents waited a day or two before they named you, who would you be just after you were born? Without a name, would you be nobody? If they had given you a different name or changed your name, would that alter who you really are? Of course not.

Are you your body? When you have a body part surgically

removed, such as your tonsils, appendix, or teeth, are you less of you? Well, physically you may be, but not actually. You're still you in there somewhere. I'd argue we're not the shell of flesh and bone that carries us around. That's just an earthly vehicle to house us for the time being.

So, are you your occupation? Relationships? Is that who you are? Are you John Smith, who works at the bank and is married to Susie Smith? Are you anyone else if you lose your job or get divorced? Again, the answer is no, that's not who you are.

None of these are you.

It looks like we've narrowed it down a bit but still haven't answered the question. Who are we, really? With several label choices safely crossed off of the list, we might turn to what's in our heads, thoughts. Sure. That's it, right? We're our thoughts. That has to be it.

Believe it or not, that's not you either. Our thoughts are just electrical pulses in a constant bouncy house inside of our head, if you will. We go about life narrating things from our perspective, creating false scenarios, trying to figure things out, and then putting them in their correct files. Thoughts shuffle around like balls in a lottery machine or bingo game, randomly colliding with each other, and, occasionally, "B-10!" pops out for an accurate thought or observation. Otherwise, the random thoughts just keep coming and jumbling together in our heads. Thoughts aren't always the same. They shift and change constantly, and they morph with our moods or physical feelings. They can also be very wrong. We may often feel like our thoughts. They're an important part of our human adventure, but they're not actually who we are. You can change your thought patterns and actions and reactions, but you still can't change you.

So apparently "you are your thoughts" isn't the answer either.

So what are you? The answer may be simpler than you think (no pun intended). Ready?

You are the one who notices and observes your thoughts and everything else around you.

That simple statement is more freeing than you imagine. For most of us, it's an entirely new concept. You see those narrating, bouncing, and sometimes annoying thoughts wandering around in your head, and observe what goes on in that bingo ball machine brain of yours. You're the one looking at them. You're the one very capable of settling those thoughts down by quieting your head as well, either by noticing the thoughts and paying no attention to them, taking action on them, or simply observing them, and letting them quietly drift by, metaphorically out your ears. THAT's who you really are. You are the one observing life passing in front of you, including all of your thoughts, because they're also part of the entire landscape you're taking in at any given time. In observing and quieting down those thoughts, we can then start to rationalize and sort through the thoughts that really matter, making better decisions and choices, experiencing life more in the moments they occur, and reducing the need for worry and stress.

Let that sink in for a moment.

Take a moment to examine everything you thought you were, but aren't. You are not fat. You may have fat, but it isn't who you are. You are not stupid. We all learn at a different level and at a different wavelength. It isn't who you are. Too many people take their identities from where they work, who they date or marry, what they own, what they look like, how much they make, their mistakes, or where they live. All of that isn't you.

So let's take what we just learned and review quickly, in a nutshell, what you are not:

your name

your body

your age

your looks or outward appearance

your car, house, or possessions

your occupation

friends or family

your mistakes

your thoughts

The spiritual teacher, Wayne Dyer paraphrased Pierre Teilhard de Chardin, when he said, "You are a spiritual being having a temporary human experience, NOT a human having a spiritual one." Whatever your beliefs may be, think about that and let it sink in for a moment as well. If you believe in heaven (or hell), your physical body doesn't continue with you. If you believe in reincarnation, you come back in a new "shell." If you believe it's simply lights out when you die, your human form is still here, just ceasing to function. The lesson in all this is that we aren't necessarily temporary and fleeting beings in spirit; we are, however, passing flesh and bone on this earth.

My take on that is, enjoy life while you're here. We weren't meant to be constantly confused, angry, or scared. In a later chapter, I'll talk about the value of suffering (yes, it has some good points). By now knowing who you really are, you can minimize or control your suffering and learn immensely from the experience.

Much of what we're capable of becoming by changing our habits or mindset comes from our awareness. Some may call it awakening to a higher reality, as when you become aware that you're dreaming in a lucid dream. When we start to notice all of the things around us, including our behaviors and beliefs, we start to wake up. When we put our phones down, walk away from the video games or boob tube, and really start paying attention to the physical world around us and what we're thinking, we start to awaken. We wake up from our dizzying day and our need for incessant distraction and entertainment. We realize that the real world isn't in an electronic device or a television show but in dealing with our fears, hopes, physical well-being, and meaningful interactions with the ones we love, (and even the ones we may not).

This is all live around us in the present moment. It isn't the past, and it isn't the future. Buddhists practice this art of living by participating in something they call mindfulness. They practice being mindful of everything they do, and you can do the same in your everyday life as well. The principle is easy, but hard to do at first. It will get easier with time and practice though. The concept of mindfulness is paying full attention to whatever you're doing, holding no judgment toward it, and letting it flow around you. Intricate tea ceremonies of Japan are an excellent example of a mindfulness exercise. It can take over an hour to perform this ceremony. It involves laying the napkins out carefully, pouring the tea very deliberately, smelling the beautiful aroma, then carefully taking that first important sip, all the while noticing everything you're touching, smelling, seeing, thinking, and experiencing. We can do this as well, with anything we choose. Try it the next time you have a simple cup of tea or even your morning coffee. Feel the warmth of the mug, smell the aroma, and see the steam slowly rising out of it. Be mindful in that present moment of the whole experience.

One of my first exercises in mindfulness happened while I was washing the dishes. I was going at the job haphazardly and was miserable in doing so. Who likes to wash the dishes anyway, right? About halfway through, I took a deep breath, relaxed, and told myself to try enjoying and fully engaging in the experience instead. And it worked! I found myself paying attention to each dish as I was cleaning it, not concentrating on the remaining dishes in the sink. I went about rubbing the washcloth with purpose around each plate and bowl. I observed how clean the dish was becoming, the smell of the dishwashing liquid, the feeling of the warm water and soap suds on my hands, and sound it made when I placed it in the drying rack. The job didn't go any quicker, but it felt like it did, and I had the added bonus of having the full experience of what it's like to do my dishes with purpose and fully enjoying it. Try it for yourself. Do it when you brush your teeth tonight or tomorrow morning. The feeling of the brush gently gliding on your teeth, the taste and smell of the toothpaste, the motion your arm makes in the process, the sound of the toothpaste when you swish it around then rinse it. Keep yourself present to what you're doing. Try not to pay attention to anything else. It may all sound foolish, but it helps to reground you in your daily life, and it helps greatly to slow your head down. It teaches you, in small batches, to fully experience and enjoy whatever you're accomplishing at the moment, and, in the bigger picture, enhances the enjoyment and experiences you have in your life in general. It also teaches an important lesson about who you really are. Remember? You're the one who notices and observes your thoughts and everything going on around you.

We seem to be losing our sense of self; many of us don't experience anything fully anymore. It all passes by us predictably as daily routines that we no longer think about or pay attention to. We then look for more tantalizing experiences to fill that void. We need a further distraction and look for future change: a different place, job, or person. When in reality, I would argue washing dishes or brushing our teeth is what real life is about. Again, it's a simple concept, but one we've strayed from. For some of us, in building sand castles and chasing brass rings toward our goals and dreams, we stopped experiencing life, simple, pleasurable life.

How many times have you left the house on your way to work and wonder, Did I remember to feed the cat, turn the stove off, or take the garbage out? We lose track of what we're doing, and because we attempt to multitask to supposedly save time, we don't know what we're doing or if we've even actually just done it!

As you start to practice mindfulness, you'll notice more around you. You'll notice things you didn't think would happen. Your mind slows down, and instead of having expectations for results of events (we'll talk about this in further detail later), you begin to accept the unfolding of things around you just as they are. The outcomes become what they are, not what we hoped or wanted them to be. You begin to notice small beauty in things you never paid attention to before, and you begin to appreciate the boring tasks you've been mindlessly trudging through in the past.

Colors become brighter, noises become more obvious, smells become more noticeable, and everything just looks different.

We're a society of people who have become mindlessly entertained. There's no substance, just mindless and pointless distraction. I also would argue that isn't what most of us really crave. Although sometimes a physiological condition, some self-induced depression's origins can often be traced back to not having a purpose. We keep looking for a bigger "point" in life, but it's often been sitting right in front of us this whole time in just brushing our teeth, and washing the dishes.

Don't let the world pass by you pointlessly. Make life purposeful in everything you do. Mindfulness is talked about a lot now, and that's not a bad thing. I think it may have lost some of its lusters, though, in the translation. I started to think of it as purposefulness instead. That connotation may help you wrap your head around the concept a little better. Concentrate on the purpose at hand. If it's washing dishes, then wash the dishes with meaning and purpose. Choose to do them or suffer the consequences of a messy kitchen, bad odor from spoiling food, or, even worse, carrying disease. You have a good reason, a purpose, for doing those dishes. Recognize it, and acknowledge it for what it is. Finding the silver lining in the most mundane of tasks in order to reframe, appreciate, and even delay gratification helps to teach us important lessons in everything we do, not just the simple duties of our day.

EXERCISE:

Take a few minutes with each of the following tasks, and purposefully accomplish them one at a time. Before you start each, answer the question: what is the purpose for doing this particular task?

When you've come up with viable reasons, answer the following questions as you're doing them: What am I feeling with my hands? Can I notice anything visually that I may have never noticed before? Are there any scents? What sounds am I hearing? Am I paying full attention to the task at hand?

Task #1 - Brush your teeth

Task #2 – Sweep the floor

Task #3 – Wash your hands

Task #4 – Make your bed

Make a mental note of the answers to all the questions asked. What were the reasons or purpose for brushing your teeth? Was it to avoid going to the dentist? The fresh feeling of clean teeth? Better breath?

As you did each task, did you notice anything you've never noticed before? The feeling of the toothbrush? The feeling of the toothpaste foam in

your mouth? The cool sensation of toothpaste on your lips? The smell of fresh mint? The sound of the bristles swishing against your teeth? Do this mental exercise for all the tasks listed, then expand to future experiences throughout the day.

As your purposefulness practice becomes routine and more habitual, begin to notice what doesn't have a purpose in your life. What is the real reason you watch the news, browse Facebook, or play video games? Are they entertaining? Sure. What's the real reason you spend so much time with them? Dig deep for this one. Are you escaping reality maybe? Are you trying to add a false sense of excitement or adventure in your life? Boost your ego? Many of us don't realize how important our lives are already, or the impact we make in the world around us. In taking your time to do our tasks purposefully, we'll also start to be mindful of the impact we make in the world around us, and the impact our actions have upon us! We'll start to realize that our actions count. People, especially children, are looking at and reacting to what we do. In raising children more effectively, it's important to pay attention to our actions more than our words. Children imitate adults. They see, and they do. The same holds true for friends and family. The people we associate with rub off on us, and conversely, we rub off on them. Our words, actions, and intentions influence them. Being purposeful helps to guide not only our actions but also the actions of everyone around us.

A very important tool in our quest for purposefulness, or mindfulness, is meditation. For some people, the image of meditation often conjures up images of yogis high upon mountain tops chanting "oohhmmm…" But that couldn't be any further from the truth. The principle behind meditation is very simple, and we can do it as an everyday practice, virtually anywhere.

Meditation enhances the concept of we are not our thoughts, we are the ones observing our thoughts we spoke about earlier. There are countless resources available to study further on meditation, and I encourage you to do so, but let me give you the basic premise of it, so you may start to reap it's benefit right now.

Meditation can be done many different ways, in many different positions, but the most common method is sitting on a cushion, legs crossed. You can also do meditation on a chair, or even laying down, if necessary. Once in a comfortable seated (or prone) position, you can either close your eyes, or keep them open. If you choose to keep them open, fix your gaze ahead of you about 5 feet. Now take a deep breath in. Your breath in should fill your abdomen, not your chest. Breath in for approximately 4-5 seconds. At the cusp of the in-breath, pause for a second or two, being mindful of the pause. Exhale for about 7 seconds, slowly, and exhaling fully. Concentrate on your breath leaving your body. Breathe in through your nose, and breathe out through your mouth. In a nutshell, that's it. It really isn't complicated, but trying to keep your mind from wandering is oh-so-hard to do!

In meditation, our goal is to quiet our mind and concentrate on our breathing. It's important that we are not attempting to control or rid ourselves of thought entirely, but to try and come to a place where your mind settles peacefully. In meditation, when thoughts arise, we notice they are there, and lovingly set them aside to continue with the practice. If a thought arises, you can gently say thinking to ourselves, and cast the thought aside, and continue concentrating on our breath.

Some people choose a mantra to concentrate on in conjunction with their breathing, for some on the in-breath they may think or feel; breathe in joy, and with the out-breath; exhale negativity. Another common mantra is let go, let God.

When we start to become mindful and more purposeful in our lives, we become happier. As we start to become happier, others naturally want to be around us more. They want to be around your vibe. They love to be in your company. Who doesn't love to be around someone who lights up the room? Some of that is their natural personality, but much of it comes from a sense that they're well grounded in reality, enjoying their life to the fullest, just as it is. People who are mindful are content with what they have. There's nothing wrong in striving to be a better person or experiencing more in life, but in order to enjoy it more, you need to be content and grateful for what you already have. Being mindful and fully present in the moment enables us to become more grateful and satisfied.

Victims of Programming and Creatures of Habit

It is extremely eye opening, and sometimes difficult, to forget what we've been taught and re-learn what we need to know. Let's think about this. Race, religious beliefs, our versions or ideas of success, the relationships with our bodies and how we think we should look when we stand in front of the mirror, how much we should earn, how big our house needs to be, bigotry, and gender inequalities are all learned. We weren't born knowing any of those, we were taught them.

I'm not saying our school, parents, or church did a less than stellar job in raising us; we were simply brought up by people who learned the same thing from their parents, instructing the same thought patterns and behaviors, passed down from one generation to the next. It created a habitual pattern of thinking about what we deem as truth. It constructs a habitual pattern about the way we act and feel about others and ourselves. Often, inadvertently, we were programmed by the people and media who surrounded us - including teachers, family, friends, television, magazines, Internet, and the radio. We obtained this vision and version of the way life should be and how we should behave from all of these outside sources.

As a society, we created religions (please note, I'm not saying anything against or for anyone's beliefs. I simply want to present these ideas, keeping an open mind about them).

These religions, in many cases, were sets of rules that dictated the behaviors of the people who followed them. Fast forward several centuries and some are still following these rules. Many of these rules are outdated, and many people don't challenge them, citing tradition. "It's the way I was taught, just like my father, and his father before him, and his father before him…" Many of the concepts and principles in religion are prudent and valuable, but I'm suggesting that it's up to each individual to sort through what's relevant in today's world, versus something that might have made sense thousands of years ago. For example, some fundamentalist Christians believe that the Earth is only several thousand years old, despite scientific evidence to the contrary. Some Muslim sects consider women inferior creatures who have no rights.

Our reaction to the events that occur in our lives, and our sense of self-worth to a certain extent, have also been taught to us. Take, for example, mistakes and failures. In today's society, mistakes, failure, and losing in general, are frowned upon. They're viewed as flaws in our character. They are, however, incredibly important factors in the progression to our growth as humans. The more discomfort we're able to press though, and the more mistakes we're allowed to make and chances to learn from them, the better we feel about ourselves. I know that sounds counterintuitive, but the better able we are to bounce back from failing or falling on our faces, the easier it is to navigate dealing with adversity in general.

The most successful people, however you look at your version of success, have made the most mistakes. I promise you that. They've created building blocks that they continually step upon to better themselves. We'll learn more about this a little later in the book.

Our support systems unwittingly taught us to learn from mistakes of successful people. That's not always a bad thing. We can gain a great amount of knowledge from those who've already made errors to give us the advantages we need today, but we still need to make our own mistakes. Understandably, parents have a hard time letting their children go through this process, because failing hurts. To put it bluntly, it just plain stinks. It's hard for a child to go through this process, but it's even harder for a parent or guardian to watch them go through it themselves. As parents, we want to coddle, to protect, and to ensure the safety of our children, both physically, and emotionally. This need for comfort and emotional sheltering could, in fact, be an enormous detriment to your children later in life, though.

Disappointment to a child can be an enormous learning tool that's vital to their growth and overall emotional well-being. In short, they need to feel uncomfortable sometimes. We all need to feel uncomfortable sometimes. A series of studies were conducted from 1960 to 1990 that are often referred to as "the marshmallow studies." In the original study, the researcher placed a marshmallow in front of several small children and told them that if they were able to wait for 15 minutes, they could have two of them instead. Many children squirmed and had a hard time resisting the treat in front of them. Some were able to, but many couldn't. For those who were able to delay their instant gratification and push through the temporary discomfort, follow-up studies found that, later in life, they scored higher on SAT tests, earned more, were less socially awkward, and had the capability of getting the hard work done.

Constant physical, emotional, and mental coddling causes a sense of entitlement. As children, many of us grew up thinking we deserve success, when, in fact, we need to earn it. Little things that go wrong during the course of the day become a big deal. We have a hard time coping because we've never actually been allowed to. We need the benefit of sporadically getting into verbal altercations at school or work. Sometimes, we need our feelings hurt, and from that, we need to learn the correct way to react, in the best, healthiest way for us to deal with it. We all know people who are on both sides of the spectrum of this. Some take rejection or a personal attack well. They brush it off, never to be thought of or spoken about again. To them, it's water under the bridge and they move on. Then there are folks who let a snide comment linger in their heads for years. They lose sleep over it, and they won't let it go and move on. They ruminate and fester over it forever. Again, I know it sounds counterintuitive, but we all need to make mistakes, we all need to feel uncomfortable, and we all need to take some lumps in life. It's actually good for us.

Does that mean I would ever accept physical abuse? Never. A consistent emotional berating? Absolutely not. Bullying has no place in my life, except to feel a sense of pity and compassion toward the aggressor (more on that later).

In our "programming" process, we lose our identity, only to take on another. This identity is something we often brand ourselves with for the rest of our lives. We pick up habits, traits, fears, and personalities from the people who surround us, and from the media. We learn social stigmas that were taught to the people who came before us. We learn how we should dress, how to act, and what to say (and when). Many of these traits are good. They help to hold the social aspect of human communication and being able to get along with one another fine, but many of these traits are arbitrary social conventions. In other words, they're ego driven, and often lack common sense.

A friend of mine was once told by a teacher that he would never be a good writer, that he should pursue other avenues for his creativity. He was told he lacked the skill necessary to be an author of any kind. He believed that lie for years. He always had the urge to write, but would soon convince himself, because of the seeds planted by that teacher, it wasn't worth it, and that he wasn't good enough. As time passed, he decided to give it a try, and low and behold, he turned out to be an incredible, inspiring author. He's published three books and is aiming to publish his forth by the middle of 2017. He pushed through the programming he had been taught, and started to think for himself.

Someone inadvertently planted the seed of doubt in his head, and he believed it. He took it as truth, but when he changed his perspective, then revisited and re-evaluated his belief about it, he discovered he's always had the talent, and the only thing holding him back was himself!

Whoever came up with the idea that women should be required to wear makeup, or men needed to wear ties, or that plaid pants are "cool," then five years later, they look ridiculous and are now "out" again? It's absurd when you think about it. With that reasoning, we should all wear togas. It was in style 2000 years ago. Wait, not anymore? Puffy dresses? No? How about powdered wigs? Anyone? I don't know; I can't keep up…. And more importantly, I (or you) shouldn't have to. Fashion changes and it's a very illogical concept to me. I label it illogical because the notion of outward beauty based on a trend or passing fad is nonsense. People follow the latest fashion trends because they want to fit in, but, more importantly, they place unnecessary stock in thinking their identity is directly related to their appearances.

So we keep repeating the same information. We pass it down to the next generation, and the media, especially mainstream news, continue to bombard us with propaganda about doom, gloom, what we need to eat, look like, and wear. It's a ridiculous notion.

Our programming also has much to do with the roles we

play in our lives and in society. These are changing though, and the past ten years has introduced more and more acceptance of multiple roles we wouldn't have seen fifty years ago. The acceptance of gay marriage or transgender rights is an example of this, as is shifting to less gender-based roles we've always accepted as normal. In the 1950s, women stayed at home, and men were the predominant breadwinners. A majority of the population went to church on Sunday (whether they truly believed in God or not) and that's all there was to that. Again, they were taught by their parents, who were taught by their parents, and so on. Women didn't have the right to vote at the turn of the 20th century and weren't allowed to participate in professional athletics, except on rare occasions such as during World War II. The lack of rights and opportunities for people of all colors over the course of American history is another prime example of the horrible prejudice and hatred that had been taught, passed down from generation to generation.

Our perceptions, more than reality, rule the way we live our lives. If we can adjust our perceptions to the way things really are, we can dramatically change our lives. Our perceptions govern everything from our concept of fear (what we're afraid of), to our self-worth. If a person suffering from low self-esteem could simply change the perception of their worth, they'd be cured. Really, it's quite that easy. However, it's also the most difficult thing in the world to do for many of us.

Our perception of fear is brought about by a series of

sources. Our parents telling us right from wrong at a young age, and those warnings to avoid heights or snakes have stuck with us. Many people have an incredibly fearful reaction to snakes because of their perceptions of them. Most snakes aren't venomous and pose no real danger to us, yet we flee in horror when confronted by the potentially harmless reptile. On the other hand, people are drawn to domestic, furry pets like cats and dogs. Yet only 5.5 people on average die each year in America from snake bites while 31 people die from dog attacks.

The media is a major perpetrator to this fear mongering. It's no secret that bad news sells, and the six o'clock news is more than happy to provide it. The truth is, we've never been healthier, lived longer, been safer, or have had so much opportunity in human history. Visit an older cemetery and note the ages of people who died during the 1700s or 1800s. It wasn't uncommon for men to have a lifespan of 40 years. Never mind the countless children who perished during plagues, polio, or tuberculosis. The numbers are staggering. In the last few years, the media has managed to whip up a frenzied fear over Ebola and the Zika viruses. Although both are serious afflictions, only four people in the United States had been infected with Ebola in 2014 and one died, and only eight people have tested positive for Zika since 2015. Hardly epidemics. Yet the news made us believe that they were. With roughly 300,000,000 humans living in the United States, the percentage of people who actually got it was unbelievably small. You had a better chance of being bitten by a shark or struck by lightning than ever getting Ebola. But the media fed on people's panic and ran with it. Our perception of the disease became warped, and we were lead to believe it was an all-out epidemic. Turns out, it wasn't even close.

Our perceptions and programming are what fuel most wars. During the Cold War against the Soviet Union from 1947 to 1991, anti-Russia propaganda was pitched to the American public, just as anti-American sentiment was pitched to the Russian people. In reality, the people of each country had more in common with each other than we thought. When the Berlin Wall finally came down, we both got a glimpse into each other's lives and found out that we all really wanted to have the same things: prosperity and safety. We thought we were fighting each other's principles as people, but it turned out to be only the governments' differences of opinions.

So what's your truth and your real story? When you essentially lay your cards on the table and look at yourself in the mirror, what is real and what have you been programmed to believe? Putting someone else's previous beliefs that you've been taught aside, what do you really believe in? What do you find to be the truth? What is the real version of the life you lead and the thoughts you think? We'll go over some more important exercises later in the book to help peel away some of these perceptions, but for now, I want you to just start thinking about being mindful in your thoughts and in your actions. I want you to start questioning the programming behind your thoughts and actions, and I want you to ask yourself often Is this really my belief, or is this something that's been taught to me?

Within our subconscious mind, we've developed a way to make our thinking process in life simpler. However, some of these simplified processes can also conjure up bad memories or emotions as well. What am I talking about here? Well, we run on a sort of an automatic pilot most days. Have you ever driven to work, like the hundreds of other times before, and never thought twice about it? We almost black out for a good portion of the trip, letting our muscle memories take over in operating the vehicle. Kind of scary, isn't it? We've evolved to use our brains on autopilot by conditioning ourselves to certain things. If we see the brake light of the car in front of us flash, we automatically step on our brake pedal.

The same process happens in bringing up some memories or emotions. People suffering from depression have this happen often when they encounter people, places, smells, etc. that remind them of the bad memories and emotion. We call these triggers. Triggers are also associated with habits or actions we do on a daily basis. Triggers can be a variety of sources, using all five senses. Have you ever smelled something familiar that transported you back in time to elementary school, or does the smell of cinnamon remind you of your grandmother's baking? Has somebody said something that conjured up a memory of a former boyfriend, or a loved one who may have passed away?

Having gone through depression, I had to take a careful look at what was triggering my negative emotions to help me gain control in avoiding or facing certain situations or people. One such trigger for me was sarcasm. Often, sarcasm is a tool that's meant to be a harmless twist on words to playfully engage someone in conversation. Unfortunately, people can also use sarcasm as a device in which to gain control or belittle another person for their own personal benefit. As a result, in order to keep myself mentally healthy, I had to separate myself from those who used extreme sarcasm as a vehicle to empower themselves, at the cost of my own dignity. The trigger of sarcasm often led to a deeper self-destruction thought pattern for me. Upon recognizing that, I was able to respond accordingly and avoid it. Often times it meant simply avoiding sarcastic people who I know would trigger me, or having a healthy sense of recognizing where and why the sarcasm was being produced.

Triggers affect our daily actions because they're automatic in nature. We don't realize they're happening. But with a little mindfulness and awareness, we can identify what triggers cause what actions and notice when those triggers start to occur. In noticing when the triggers start to occur, we can help control the actions we don't want to happen such as eating when we feel bored or shopping when we feel bad about ourselves.

EXERCISE:

This exercise will help you to gain control or, at least, help you to manage some of your triggers and unwanted actions. Take a piece of paper and make five columns. Label the first "I'd like to change," the second "what's the root cause," the third "the trigger," the fourth "my epiphany," and the fifth, "action plan."

In the first column, list some of the habits or traits you'd like to change such as lose weight, spend less, quit smoking, or use less social media. In the second column, take the time to find a reason why you're doing what you're doing. Is it boredom? Fear? Lack of attention? In the third column, write the trigger that may have steered you to think about doing what you didn't want to do. Did you see a television commercial with a person who looked a certain way? Did you see a photo that reminded you of an old boyfriend or girlfriend? Did you hear an old song that conjured up some old feelings or emotions? In the fourth column, write your epiphany. Take a big step back from yourself and look at the habit objectively, and tell the truth about it. I'll use Facebook (or social media in general) as an example. "Facebook likes are not real attention or love." "People are really only posting the good in their lives, but aren't that happy in real life." "Facebook is a series of people's greatest hits." "When I think about my old boyfriend or girlfriend, I get lonely and need the fleeting attention social media provides." Then in the fifth column, come up with an action plan that will help steer you away from that action. For example, turn off your notifications and start socializing with people face-to-face instead of Facebook-to-Facebook, or avoid triggers such as looking at old photos of boyfriends or girlfriends past who may instill a feeling of being unloved or lonely.

Please keep in mind, this isn't a failsafe method to end all of your bad habits or identify all triggers. Some of the triggers may be very deep-seated and require the help of a professional therapist to dig up the root causes. But, for some habits, this simple exercise may help you to realize some of their root causes. You may have never realized that you're on Facebook so much because you're bored or feel unloved, and you think the "likes" of Facebook are helping to give you the positive attention you crave (the science behind Facebook and the little red notification symbols alone could easily fill a book). Maybe you have FOMO (fear of missing out).

When you notice why you were triggered toward Facebook, or are already on it, turn to your action plan to back away. That action plan may consist of

a host of solutions, including (but not limited to) taking a walk, doing yoga, meditating, calling a friend, visiting a family member, or writing. If you determined that you use Facebook because you feel isolated or lonely, then your action plan may be to call or visit a friend or family member. If it's out of boredom, then your action plan may be to take a walk, read a book, or do some journaling.

The idea is to try to catch the trigger before the action begins. This will be difficult at first, but becomes easier with time. Then, eventually becomes a normal habit for you.

Recognizing and controlling those triggers helps us to regulate our actions. As you're going for that bowl of ice cream, you can stop, with the spoon in the container, ready to scoop some out, and think, Wait. Every time a see a photo of a thin woman, I think, "what's the use, I'll never look perfect, so why try?" Then create an action plan to rectify both the future trigger and the action that would have followed. "I need to stop looking at magazines or television programs that flaunt false images of the 'perfect' looking woman. Instead of eating ice cream, I'll journal about ten things I'm grateful for or call a friend who can cheer me up and make me feel better about myself." In moving forward with some of the same concepts in this book, take the same steps when you notice yourself expressing what may be limited beliefs about someone, feeling like buying something you don't need, or lingering on social media too long.

Our perceptions are essentially the stories we tell ourselves about anything. In taking the time to dissect them a bit, we learn a new story. That's what we're trying to accomplish here, really. We've been told by others or have taught ourselves a certain story about who we are and how we should act, but we need to rewrite the story of our thinking and our lives.

Working on these stories and preconceived ideas are not impossible, but the ingrained thoughts can be difficult to change because it's not always easy to work on the parts of us that don't get applause. Because our attention-seeking boundaries are often out of sync, we avoid doing what we need to do to make ourselves grow.

Ego – Am I Winning? Who's Keeping Score?

There's a potentially insidious enemy lurking around every corner that craves attention, respect, greed, power, recognition, and will often go wild with abandon if not properly kept in check. It has ruined countless lives and broken marriages. It has caused wars, and millions of people have perished because of this horrible thing. It is a creature that lurks within all of us.

This seemingly horrible monster is actually a very tameable, and potentially loveable thing called ego.

Ego is the part of us that, for our early ancestors, was often the difference between life and death. Remember survival of the fittest from Chapter 1? Well, this is where ego played an integral part of our well-being. Our craving for competitive victories, being top dog, as it were, and keeping up with the Joneses are all derived here. They certainly had a place when your life depended on it, and there was a time when it meant a rising of the leader of the pack.

When we say someone hurt our feelings, we often really mean someone bruised our ego. We were challenged somehow, and we lost or had the perception of losing. Not winning stays in our gut, often making us feel like we're no longer in charge, inferior, unloved, or somehow less of a human.

When people think of ego, though, they generally produce images of someone who's egotistical, who's full of themselves or arrogant. But ego itself, when portrayed that way, often means a deficiency of ego within. Ego is the cause of our guilt and fears of rejection. It's the cause of our feeling less than we are and our making others feel less than they are. Why would we want to make another feel less than they are? So we can feel better about ourselves, and therefore, raise our own ego. Sounds like a giant horrible cycle, right? Well, it is. Left unchecked, it keeps growing and growing and growing.

Because of its importance in the need for survival thousands of years ago, it has evolved into something different, especially in the technological age. Our bragging rights used to be based on our abilities to stay alive and actively contribute to a community or group. We were accepted, based on our survival skills. Now, our egos are based more on physical beauty, wealth, power, or recognition. What kind of attention we can muster up through social media and the Internet. YouTube or Facebook alone has had the ability to create stars from unknown people almost overnight. Reality TV shows such as Survivor, American Idol, So You Think You Have Talent, and The Voice take relatively unknown people and create celebrities out of them. We seem to be on a constant quest for fame, for being the best, for showcasing our talents, and for winning, and in this age of being socially connected, we want everyone to see it. And if we don't want to be the active celebrity, we at least want to live vicariously through their successes, talent, and power. We hold admiration for and identify with those who are often in the spotlight.

It seems like many of us has a constant need for competition. I haven't even begun to introduce the concept of professional sports. We idolize, cheer, and spend hard-earned time and money to watch grown men and women play a predesigned game with inflated balls, sticks, goals, and nets. They're all played on predetermined playing fields, and are all limited in their time to calculate who won. And we love it. We idolize the better players, often regardless of their personal lives, and put them on pedestals to worship. The same often goes for actors and musicians. We hold them to a standard that isn't our own, and base our admiration on how famous or well known they are. The problem with this "fame" recognition or idolatry is that it's empty. It's trying to catch the brass ring that always seems to be one step ahead of us, always elusive, always just out of our grasp. And you know what? It will always be so. Some things our minds create weren't meant to be achieved. I honestly believe in raising the bar to better ourselves, but there's also such a thing as setting unrealistic, and unachievable goals.

Ego is an odd trait we've evolved into. Essentially, in this modern age, ego is a form of insanity. It's a trick our minds play on us. Ego isn't a tangible, touchable thing. It's merely an instinctive concept that many of us don't even know we have. On the grand scale of things, the ego can range from the suicide fueled "I'm pathetic; the world would be better off without me" to the narcissistic notion that "I'm God's gift to the human race; I'm simply better than everyone." Ego has driven people to actually take their own lives, been the cause of many wars, and ruined countless lives. Ego is what drives us to sometimes do unspeakable horrors, and it can control us far more than we all care to admit. Not bad for an intangible, untouchable concept our minds have created, right? Ego is the force behind greed, and the catalyst for a lot of our self-worth or, more importantly, lack of it. It is also predominately the burden of the youth. Luckily, it seems that as we get older, many of us start to lessen the impact and stranglehold that ego has on us from years of conditioning. You often hear of people softening and becoming more gentle and compassionate as they get older. We start to realize that we don't really need the coolest pair of sneakers or the flashiest car. I think as we grow older, ego wears out its welcome. We begin to realize that our time could have been better spent, we start to face our own mortalities, and we begin to settle into the notion that it's now better to diminish our need for outward competition and concentrate on competing to make ourselves better humans. I think we start to make friends with our ego as we mature, and after years of suffering and fighting it, we embrace the lessons it has taught us, and sigh over the hell it occasionally put us through.

Ego is the mind-made self that was created from your early environment and the way you were raised. Ego, to us, is as real as something in front of us. It's the thought patterns and processes with which we cling to life itself. People suffering severe depression have the capability to end their own lives based simply on the notion that they're not satisfying their ego. They kill themselves based on a concept that's not based on reality. In the last chapter, we spoke about creating a new story. These people had written horror stories about themselves and were unable to process the information around them correctly to write new stories. They had such a low sense of themselves because they based much of it on a comparison to others. But as with most things that are based on greed or fleeting materialism, the ego is also incredibly and surprisingly fragile. It doesn't take much to upset the ego, which is why it gets us into half the problems and issues in our lives.

Ego stems from a scarcity mentality. It thinks there's never enough. There's never enough love, money, pride, or beauty. And with that scarcity mentality, it makes us feel as though we're lacking as human beings. Let me reveal the real answer right here very plainly. As human beings, none of us lack. We're all uniquely and beautifully perfect. Only our minds sometimes refuse to believe that. On the other end of the spectrum, the scarcity mentality in some people causes them to have a superiority complex. Thus, they lift themselves up by knocking others down. This is a common trait of narcissists, autocratic bosses, and dictators. They raise their own personal and social status by dropping everyone else's. Freedoms and privileges are stripped away. Adolf Hitler is a prime example of someone who was so insecure that he let his ego run rampant, senselessly executing millions of humans, essentially to benefit himself.

Do any humans lack anything? Of course, some do such as starving people in third world countries and the homeless in developed countries. Children are abused and unloved every day, and freedoms have been stripped from many. However, we're still all the same beautifully and wonderfully created humans, plain and simple, regardless of age, sexual orientation, skin color, religion, culture, language, heritage, living conditions, or social status.

Nothing strengthens the ego more than being right. And for many, their sense of right is the only way. There's an old saying that goes, "Sometimes, it's better to be kind than right." I believe that to be the case many times.

Now that I've gotten the negative connotations of ego out of the way, let me introduce some good, and healthy points about it. Ego, when tamed, and in check, is a wonderful and necessary tool in our growth as humans. The need to win, as I portrayed earlier, is also not always detrimental. The need to win, in a healthy ego, has more to do with the need for conquering ourselves or the need for the betterment of others. Healthy competition also prepares us for losing, an important part of life that carries on to so many other areas of our lives. A person with a healthy ego is able to separate what people say to them from the person saying it. They can accept the challenges and rejections life will hand them, and they look for better ways to continue challenging themselves.

In closing this chapter, I want to leave you with a few thoughts for dealing with the ego, both yours and that of others, to help ease the pain and need for our egos to continue being fed.

Is your current social media status based upon your ego? Are you celebrating your "life's greatest hits" on it? Are you constantly checking your electronic devices for notifications? Are you afraid if you don't keep in constant contact with the world via your phone, you're somehow missing out on life?

Plan a media-free day soon. Pick a date, let your friends and family know that you'll be unplugging, and then go off the grid for 24 hours. Let yourself squirm, then enjoy the feeling of freedom you get in turning things off for a while. Plan lots of fun things to do, either by yourself or with others, on that day not only to help ease the burden of being offline but also to experience life without thinking you need to announce what you're doing or know what everyone else is doing that day.

Another great suggestion is to pick a friend and either call them or plan a coffee date. Be mindful during the conversation about what you say, and how you react to their side of the conversation. Purposefully steer the conversation away from yourself, and find ways to encourage and listen to your friend, offering a kind word or asking good questions to keep the conversation engaged more toward making them feel better, instead of yourself.

As was said earlier, by being mindful and watching for triggers, we can curb our ego and let it rest when needed.

And that's a vacation that all of us should take on a regular basis by subsiding our egos and resting our weary spirits. We don't always need to win. Sometimes letting someone else take home the trophy is winning in another way.

False Expectations. Looking at Life as It Is, Rather Than as You Think It Should Be

The Buddhists believe the cause of all suffering comes from the concept of things not turning out the way we hoped or thought they would. We hold a certain set of expectations that govern our moods. We have certain rules and think a certain way, and if those expectations aren't met, we suffer. We pout, stamp our feet, cry, and get upset. Just look at rush hour traffic to put that notion to the test. We're running late, and we gripe, "If only people would drive better. Construction? You've got to be kidding me! This wasn't supposed to be that way!"

Having false expectations is the reason you allow other people to hurt you. Yes, unfortunately, I did say allow. This just in—just because you're nice to someone or go out of your way for them, doesn't mean they'll like you back, or treat you right with the dignity you think you deserve. It doesn't mean they'll treat you the way you treated them. You expect more from them, and when those expectations are broken or fall short, you get genuinely upset. "How could they do this to me? I was SO good to them!" I EXPECTED them to _____ (fill in the blank). They should have _____ (fill in the blank). I thought they were going to _____ (fill in the blank). This is the way many of us think and act. But if we're able to just accept things as they happen, to let life simply unfold as it happens, imagine the peace we would have. Can you imagine how good you would feel if you did something nice for someone else, simply out of love with no expectations of a return favor or no expected results?

We have an enormous illusion that we're somehow in control of everything around us. That would be a very inaccurate assumption, to say the least. Sure, things often happen in the order and manner they should, and, sometimes, we're able to reign in people to act in certain ways to appease our moods or idiosyncrasies for the moment. But, ultimately, we don't have control of the people, situations, timing, or weather in our lives. Things happen. Plans take a left when you want to turn right. But you know what? That's okay. It's alright, really. Letting go of expectations from people, from life, and from yourself is a good thing. That doesn't mean to say we don't need goals and dreams, those are very important for our well-being. What I'm saying is to bend with those goals and dreams.

Things simply won't always go according to plans. There, I said it. You can count on that, too. How you react to those changes and shifts will determine whether you find peace or experience frustration. Life goes on, the way it wants to, and there's not a damn thing you can do about it. This another very freeing concept once you are able to digest it.

So here's a suggestion. Why not go with the flow? Have you ever gotten married or gone on a big vacation and something out of the ordinary happened? Whether good or bad, I bet it was the moment you remembered most about the whole thing. It made that event in your life that much more memorable. Treat life and the moments contained within it as an adventure. It rains, luggage gets lost, meals get screwed up, cars break down, and again, people don't do or act the way you'd like them to. Roll with it. Smile at it. Embrace it and accept it. It sounds easy, right? Well, obviously, if it were, we'd all be doing it. But it is possible to shift your mindset to accept life exactly as it unfolds. We've all met people like that. They know how to roll with the punches and get up when they get knocked down. We often refer to them as strong, when, in fact, they're just able to adapt much easier. And you know what? They're probably the happiest people we know. When we drop our rigid expectations about the way life should happen, another wonderful concept is introduced into our lives. Because we drop the expectation, our perspective shifts to the outlook that everything is unfolding just the way it should be.

EXERCISE:

Here are two exercises to help you drop the expectations of the way you think things should be, and to help you go with the flow.

1. Do something out of the ordinary to force yourself into an unexpected situation. I don't mean anything dangerous or illegal, obviously. But just put your foot in the water to see how you'll react. Put yourself to the test a bit and be very mindful of what you're going through, and what you feel. Be

extra nice to someone, expecting nothing in return. Talk to a difficult neighbor, or bring them a gift. Take note, smile at it, and see if you can lean into it, and attach a new perspective to it that it's just life, and you have no control over it. Let it take you there, let it roll off of your back, and try to roll with the punches. Think of it like a seagull sitting in the ocean. When a wave comes (unexpected events in life we have little control over) the seagull simply floats upward with the wave, until it passes, and it just settles back down to where it was before. No big deal, no big production, no worry, anger, or sweat.

2. The next time you find life getting rocky, instead of blaming the circumstances, look at why things unfolded the way they did. As I've discussed earlier, this is a great opportunity to change your perspective, and tell yourself what the true story is.

Let me give you an example. I gained this epiphany a few years ago when I was driving to work in heavy traffic and found myself livid at the cars around me. THEY were the reason I was going to be late! I was stressed and anxious. Then it dawned on me. I had left at the last minute, leaving only minimal time to spare. I also didn't bother to listen to traffic reports so I could potentially avoid the congested area. It wasn't the fault of everyone around me after all, was it? It was my own creation. When I discovered that small fact, I was

both embarrassed and enlightened. There's another old saying that goes, "Some people create their own storms, then cry when it rains." How true is that statement for you? Next time you're upset that circumstances may not have turned out the way you wanted, peel back the layers and find out why it didn't. Was it, in fact, you who sabotaged yourself?

Having gone through major depression, I found that it's a disease that plays tricks with your head. You honestly believe the world would be better without you and that, in some cases, everyone was out to get you. The biggest underlying symptom and problem with depression is a negative outlook, whether self-created or not. Even without depression, most of us still operate with a negative perspective on the events and people around us. We believe the worst and expect the worst in everything. Our expectations are often met because we create what we think about and we've lowered our standards so much.

So are we in control of anything in our lives? No. We do, however, have a very high percentage of things that turn out exactly as planned, though. Much of our expectations have to do with our brains keeping a track record of the way things have turned out in the past and assuming they will again. When these outcomes don't match exactly with what the brain thinks they should be, we get confused and our egos get bruised. When things don't turn out the way we want, it's almost like losing. Remember the competitive edge and the need to win that we talked about earlier? Many of these outcomes are actually great learning experiences, but we view them as burdensome because they aren't our outcomes. We feel a sense of freedom has been stripped from us the minute the outcomes are not of our making. Driving your car to work is a conscious choice. Having it break down isn't. If you're able to accept the fact that your car broke down the day and time it did, it becomes easier to deal with it. Once you accept that things happen with no rhyme or reason sometimes, within the scope of possibilities, you're able to just see it unfold in front of you. You didn't, in fact, lose, and your freedom isn't in danger. Things just turned out differently, that's all. People didn't act the way you expected them too, and friends or family didn't do things the way you thought they should do them.

As some of us choose to trudge through life, and that's probably not a bad description for many, we narrate it constantly in our ever-active mind. We also subconsciously attach meanings and outcomes to all of it. "She should have... He should have... They should have... I should have..." We give fuel to our ego by hoping things will turn out a certain way, and constantly disappointing ourselves over and over and over again when the outcome doesn't turn out to our liking.

Life shouldn't be about trudging through it. It should be about observing and accepting it. Things are going to happen a certain way based on timing and how your plans interact with everyone else's, and there's no way we can control or foresee what will happen. Once we start wrapping our thoughts around that, we start to gain more control over our sanity and live a more stress-free existence. We need to grasp the reality that we are, indeed, not in control of the universe.

As we become more accepting of the way things are versus how we want them to be, we start to change the way we also look at ourselves. We begin to accept ourselves as well. We begin to see ourselves in a different light. I've known so many men who, upon the thinning of their hairlines, start doing these ridiculous comb-overs to compensate for their new lack of hair. They haven't accepted the fact that they are indeed getting older. Or if starts to turn gray, many of us fight it with dyes. Have you noticed that those who accept that they're getting older and move on are the happiest?

There comes a time where we simply need to accept ourselves as we are: warts, lumps, mistakes, and all. I can assure you that you'll feel relief when you finally are free of most of your preconceived notions of who you should be. What I'm suggesting here is keeping a realistic version of self-improvement. Should you run out to buy hair dye or a toupee when your hair goes south? I think that's a personal choice, but I would say that's a battle not worth fighting. It's another of society's tricks in making us think that when we become old (heaven forbid!), we're not as relevant. Choose your battles wisely, and work on something that will benefit yourself and the world in bigger ways than your hair.

Another issue we face with the personal expectation "things didn't turn out the way I planned" problem is one of the biggest traps we'll ever fall into in our lives. It's the "I'll be_____ when _____" trap. You know, I'll be happy when I lose ten pounds. I'll be satisfied when I get that promotion, I'll be complete when I meet that perfect person. I'll be justified when karma has its way. This game we play with ourselves keeps us on a constant hamster wheel, letting time slip by minute by minute, never being happy in the now.

These thought patterns and processes are also linked to the notion that our happiness is directly dependent on other people. When he or she does this, then I'll be happy. If he or she would stop doing this, then I'll be happy.

I've got news for you. Your happiness is your choice. I know that's an incredibly simplistic statement, but, for many, it's one they've never heard or even thought about. Think about that. You can choose to be happy at any moment. Your reaction to any event, to other people, to your job, to anything is your decision. The problem is we have that automatic trigger (remember that?), which says, if someone says or does X, then I react with Y. It's an automatic reflex that we lock into. It can be changed, though. Our thinking can be changed. Similar to Chapter 3's exercise, find out what makes you unhappy. Make a list of those things, and come up with an action plan to combat those triggers. When you find your spouse bringing up your mother, which always ticks you off, notice it, then have a plan ready. If you haven't got an action plan, go back to chapter 3, and put it through the exercise found there. For most of us, that would serve us and the people around us better. Take a deep breath and let it go.

In all of this, we need to tell ourselves a new story. We've gone over this in Chapter 3, but the concept remains the same. Adjust your perceptions on the situation, lay your cards on the table, look at yourself in the mirror, and tell yourself the truth. After you hash that out, tell yourself a new story. Rewrite what needs to be revised. Be honest with yourself.

EXERCISE:

I want you to choose three things you fear or even things that you've been worrying about lately. On a piece of paper, make five columns. Label each column: 1) Fear, 2) Reason, 3) Worst-Case Scenario, 4) Most Likely Realistic Outcome, 5) Freedom. In the first column, I want you to make a list of your three fears or worries. They can be anything from bunny rabbits to public speaking, to flying in an airplane or even starting a new job. Go ahead; list them. Feel free to add more if you'd like, but name at least three. In the second column, I want you to think hard and write the reason you have that fear. Any reason that comes to mind. In the third column, write down the worst-case

scenario that could happen, and in the fourth column, write down the real probable outcome that would happen. Think hard; this is the part when you need to be very realistic about this. When you start breaking down some of these imaginings and feelings, you can begin to understand how our preprogrammed thoughts about these fears can start to change. Are some fears valid? Absolutely. Are most? Absolutely not. Look at your list, and based upon the probable outcomes, ask yourself why you're so afraid of that thing or situation. In the fifth column, I want you to write the epiphany you've concluded about your fear to gain your freedom from it. Let me give you an example; let's say my fear is public speaking. In the following five columns, I may write the following:

1) Fear – Public speaking

2) Reason – Possible embarrassment and anxiety

3) Worst-case scenario – I totally forget what I have to say, and I stand up there looking like a fool, saying nothing.

4) Most likely, realistic outcome – I'm nervous, but manage to say what needs to be said, making a few mistakes along the way, from which I can probably recover.

5) Freedom – I will not die giving this presentation, and the audience will be more than empathetic

since they would be just as frightened doing the same thing. As long as I'm well-rehearsed in my presentation and knowledgeable about the subject matter, it will go just fine. It's just a presentation. In the grand scheme of things, this isn't life or death. My getting through this will gain me both experience and confidence in giving future presentations and tackling other tough obstacles in life.

To summarize, when we expect events to turn out the way we want and people to act the way we want them to, we're guaranteed to be very disappointed. Live with the fact that things will often turn out close to the way you imagined, but be open to and accepting of the possibility that they may not, and that's perfectly okay.

In closing the chapter, I'd like to ease some of the burdens of your expectations in life by going over a few things you are responsible for, and a few things you are not;

You are responsible for;

Your actions and reactions.

Your thoughts.

Your own happiness.

Communicating effectively (what you say, and how you say it).

You are not responsible for;

Other people's actions or reactions.

Other people's feelings.

Other people's happiness.

Other people's perceptions of the way life should be (or is).

Knowing some of these simple responsibilities can make an enormous difference in the way you approach your perspective and emotions, and frees you from the responsibility of feeling you have to constantly "fix" it in others.

Emotions – Unrealistic Feelings of Regret, Rejection, Shame, Fear, Unworthiness, Pride, and Guilt

In our caveman or cavewoman brain mode (instinct/fight or flight/survival of the fittest), the need for survival depended on several factors, including our need to belong or, more importantly, our usefulness to the tribe. It was only in working together, doing their jobs, that everyone survived. That need is still there, but conditions and situations have changed. We still depend on others for food production and the manufacturing of goods necessary to our well-being but not in the same way. Our subconscious brains, however, don't know that. They simply haven't evolved enough to accept this. So, we still have the extreme need and longing to belong, and in that need, we have what feels like a genuine struggle for survival. In other words, if we don't fit in, we subconsciously feel that we could die.

In this longing to belong or fit in, we encounter almost countless challenges rooted in the way we were raised. Pleasing parents and teachers early on in our lives continue to haunt us in our jobs, marriages, and friendships. When we want to please but feel as though we've fallen short, we feel shame, guilt, and fear that we'll be rejected or unworthy. We feel like our very survival is at stake.

In most cases, we can lump such emotions into one. Although we give different names to them, they still mean basically the same thing and are brought about by the same process. That process is a low self-worth. Think about that. People who experience higher levels of anxiety, regret, guilt, shame, and unworthiness, all have the same basis of thought. We feel we don't measure up to other peoples' standards. We need to please. We need to feel important, loved, and appreciated. We want to be recognized and validated. Those people who feel the unrealistic pull of those emotions are craving the need to fit in. Simple, unintended rejection feels catastrophic and can come in many different forms. It could be simply not recognizing something; "She ate the dinner I cooked, and didn't even say she liked it. She must hate it, and she must hate me!" It could also come in the forms of sarcasm or constructive criticism.

When we're rejected because of slights or criticism, we overreact to somehow reason that if they don't like what I did or said, they obviously don't like me, and if they don't like me, then I'm not a good person. Can you see the correlation here? If we break apart this series of thinking, it almost seems ridiculous, but when you're going through it, it certainly doesn't feel ridiculous. It's also the way we think, and we're triggering ourselves (remember those again?) back into feeling all kinds of uncomfortable emotions we don't want.

Don't get me wrong; there are good places for some of these emotions. A child who's done something wrong should have a healthy feeling of remorse or guilt. Parents, be careful in the way you present the concept of guilt to your child, though. A healthy sense of remorse is developed in a child's healthy sense of empathy. A child should be taught to feel guilty when he or she has made a mistake that directly correlates to a misdeed like stealing, lying, or physical violence toward another person. They need to be taught that those are disrespectful and hurtful actions that negatively affect other people. The wrong triggering sense of remorse is imposed when parents do this for their own sense of control and ultimate selfish benefit. When guilt is used as a form of punishment, you could be doing more harm than good!

As we learned earlier, the need to please and feel loved is an instinct that evolved over tens of thousands of years. This is why what other people's thoughts and expectations matter so much. Some of the most guilt-provoking words anyone can say to another are "I'm disappointed in you" or "you let me down." We feel a need to live up to what others expect of us. This isn't always detrimental though. Sometimes, we're able to become a better person when someone holds a higher standard for us than we hold for ourselves. Be careful with this, however, because people can also have the wrong or impossible goals or standards for others, and their love or approval may be contingent on the accomplishment of that goal or standard. For example, a father who's a doctor may expect his son to follow in his footsteps. But the son wants to be an artist. Separate the expectations from what a person really is, both in setting goals and standards for others, in setting them for yourself, and when people set them for you. Remember, we spoke about labels, and who you really are earlier? Your accomplishments or achieved status in anything isn't who you are; it's what you do or have done. There's a big difference. Remember that.

One of the key elements in dealing with our emotions is being careful not to lay the blame upon anyone else for our reactions. That is still ours to choose, always. Even if our circumstances are dire or horrific, we can always choose our reaction. Dr. Viktor Frankl wrote about this concept in more detail in Man's Search for Meaning. Dr. Frankl was a Jewish psychologist who was sent to a concentration camp during World War II. Most of his family were killed or separated from each other. The living conditions in the camp were deplorable. Starving and often naked, Frankl didn't know if he would be executed or when his next meal was. Even in all of this unspeakable horror, Dr. Frankl still maintained the morale of the other prisoners, and even some of the guards. How did he do this? By not giving up the one thing he still had a choice in the matter over, his attitude. He knew he was still responsible for how he reacted to all of the carnage that surrounded him in the concentration camps. Frankl went on to teach about this after his release from the camp and is an example of fortitude and what the human mind is capable of, keeping a positive, hopeful attitude and outlook even in the most horrific situations.

We're the ones who eventually allow our emotions to spiral out of control or exaggerate our thinking, not other people.

Having worked in a retail management position for well over twenty-five years, my secret weapon against an irate customer was always peace. I would always listen carefully, not speaking, then calmly answer back restating facts, separating what was their opinion from reality. More often than not, the customer would start to feel embarrassed or silly in their behavior, and calm down themselves. They had whipped themselves into a virtual frenzy over a little misunderstanding, or miscommunication, mostly made up in their minds.

I always liked the "farmer and the jack" parable. The story goes that a young couple had broken down with a flat tire in front of a farmhouse in the country. Upon trying to change the flat tire, the young man notices he doesn't have a car jack to lift the car up. His wife suggests they go up to the farmhouse and ask if they might have one they can borrow. They start walking toward the house, and the young man says, "Of course they have a jack, it's a working farm. Of course, they'll let us use it." They continue walking a little further, and the young man, with his mind working overtime says, "You know, he probably has a jack, but what if he doesn't let us use it?" "You're being silly," his wife says. They walk a little further, coming closer to the door, and the young man announces, "You know, I bet they have a jack, but won't let us use it. I bet they won't care we're broken down. I bet they're too stingy to lend it out." They approach the front door and knock. An elderly, kind farmer opens the door with a broad smile, and asks, "Hello, may I help you?" The young man then proclaims, "Yeah, take your jack and shove it; I didn't want to use it anyway!"

How many times have we festered, flip flopped, and rumbled around all these thoughts in our head, only to unload on an oftentimes very unsuspecting victim in a barrage of accusations, and falsehoods that we managed to conjure up, and kept us sleepless for the last several nights. Meanwhile, they had no ill intentions or knew you felt this way. They're shocked and surprised at such an unusual conclusion.

When we resent, are hurt, jealous, envious, or angry – we often create a story. Be cautious and truthful what story you are telling yourself about the circumstances at hand.

We do this to ourselves as well. We beat ourselves up repeatedly for a past infraction, something that we said or did years ago. We bounce these negative, self-defeating thoughts around in our heads like bees in a beehive, shaking it up, we get it (ourselves) angrier and angrier.

A good way to look at the effectiveness of this negative thought pattern we subject ourselves to is to picture a small child. Picture this as carefully as you can. This adorable, innocent, lovable child is maybe seven or so years old. Picture yourself yelling at this child, telling them that they're no good, that they should have never been born. Call them the stupidest person alive, and tell them they mean nothing. Tell them they have no purpose and have no place in this world.

Did you picture it? How did it make you feel? Like a heel or an incompetent adult, right? Can you imagine how it made the child feel? Worthless, unloved, and probably sobbing at the tirade you just let loose on them. The point is if you wouldn't talk to a child that way, why would you consider doing the same to your own inner child?

We don't realize it, but, for many of us, that self-effacing and deprecating speech is common when we "talk" to ourselves. When we make a mistake, say the wrong thing, or spill something, often, the first thing that comes to mind is "I'm clumsy," "How stupid was that?" "I can't believe I did that," or "I'm a complete idiot." Stop it. Be mindful of the action, notice your thinking, then reframe the situation and rewrite the story. I'm not dumb. I did something that may not have been wise, but I'm separate from the event. Smart people do foolish things sometimes. Learn the lesson; move forward.

Our Want for Comfort, the Value in Feeling Uncomfortable

Part of the progression we've made as humans had a lot to do with our need for both survival and comfort (safety). They've been at the forefront of our development. Unfortunately, the need for safety has caused many of us to burrow our heads in the sand to avoid unpleasantness at any cost. We sit inside, watching television, and what little time we do spend out and about, we're so busy checking our social media, YouTube, emails, or playing games on our phones, we miss out on what's in front of us. We've gone to many lengths to smooth out the highs and lows of life, so that it's become one safe life with no ups or downs. We've lost the need for challenge, and, more importantly, we've lost the real need for discomfort.

Discomforts are important. They remind us that we need to embrace it all in our lives. Both the good and the bad. Because no matter what, the bad will happen. Putting ourselves through discomfort to get to the other side is also good for us, because it offers perspective. We aren't so upset about the bad things that happen in our daily routines, because we realize it isn't all that big a deal after all. The programmed, triggered responses start to fade away. When we subject ourselves to more discomfort, we're actually able to feel less discomfort in the long run.

I'm a hiker who has no problem getting dirty on the

mountain trail. I find it kind of fun. I have, however, taken folks hiking with me who are literally scared to death of getting dirty, of actually getting some mud on their boots. They're afraid of falling, crossing an easy brook and getting a little wet if their foot slips into it. As children, we're taught by our parents not to do certain things for our own safety and protection, including, for some reason, getting wet. May I make a suggestion to any parents of younger children out there? Let them jump in mud puddles. It's good for them. Teach them the genuinely bad stuff to stay away from, but let them get messy. May I make another suggestion to all adults out there? You should also jump in mud puddles. It's good for you.

We need to stop embracing our fear of getting uncomfortable. I mean this in so many different ways such as in our emotions, relationships, jobs, or physically. There's something to be said about getting muddy, filthy, wet, and dirty. We run like people possessed when it's raining out, afraid of getting wet, or messing up our hair. Yet we spend 15 minutes in a shower, enjoying every second of it. Why are we so afraid to get wet or dirty?

Some folks are bucking the trend toward comfort and pushing their physical limits when it comes to challenging themselves in new ways. Behold the Spartan and Tough Mudder races. These are Army boot camp style races that drag it's participants through mud, barbed wire, confined spaces, freezing cold water, dirt, grime, and ladders. Doing these tough challenges helps to make what we consider "problems" pale in comparison. It gives perspective. No, they're not for everyone. You run twelve miles though fire, mud, and freezing water; climb rope ladders; carry logs up mountains; and crawl on your belly under barbed wire. After running a race like that, when the coffee isn't hot enough, you encounter some traffic, or your pen runs out of ink, you're okay with that. No catastrophe. You'll be alright, honest. Perspective.

Here are some suggestions for getting us out of our comfort zones, and feeling a little uncomfortable;

- Tell someone you've never said it to before that you love them.
- Write someone a heartfelt letter about the impact they've made in your life, especially someone who may not expect it.
- Eat something new.
- Jump in the puddles. I know you're an adult, but do it anyways.
- Take a long walk in the rain.
- Take a cold shower.
- Go someplace you've never been.
- Go play in the dirt. Get muddy.
- Take on a race or physical challenge (Spartan Race, Tough Mudder, or a walkathon if you're not in

shape).

- Say hello to strangers.

- Ask a stranger out. Ask them for a date, just for coffee. Whatever.

These are just a few simple examples, but there are literally millions more you can engage in.

By stretching our comfort zones, we learn to eventually feel less fear, which leads us to feeling less stressed and more human. Animals have a way of taking the fight or flight action, then letting it go. When you see a squirrel being chased by a cat, there's a genuine risk that it could be lunch if caught. But give it a little while, and the squirrel is back in the same place, doing the same thing before the cat came. We have much better memories than a squirrel, but need to let more go. Once the danger has passed, learn your lesson, and brush it off. There are people who are afraid of dogs, for example, who were bitten by one when they were young, and they still hold that fear today. We have a hard time letting go of what we've experienced or been taught when young.

Watching television is easy. No need to get dirty, and no need for anyone to see us. We can live and feel vicariously through the actors on the screen. Instead of getting dirty and bloody in a Spartan or Tough Mudder race, we let Bruce Willis do it in a Die Hard movie. We're comfortable pretending we're someone else.

As humans have evolved, we've found many ways to take the pain of life away. We think that in taking away pain, our lives get better, but the opposite is often true. I should clarify that when I speak of pain, I'm speaking of our discomfort. Not only in the obvious, such as speaking in front of a large group of people, or in grieving the death of a loved one, but some less obvious discomforts, like social interaction and dealing with real life, basic events as they happen. Much of our perceived comfort actually comes from creating distractions to life, instead of facing it. These distractions have increased dramatically over the last fifty years, and have bombarded us like the human race has never seen in the last five to ten.

The main distraction and obvious culprit is technology. Although made to make our lives better, it's doing quite the opposite. Our attention spans have grown shorter, our gratitude toward simple and beautiful things has waned, and our communication with each other has become remote and disjointed instead of face-to-face and present.

We now create personas online on such social media platforms as Facebook, Instagram, and Twitter. As these addictive and often misrepresented platforms gain popularity, there doesn't seem to be any limit to the creation and use of them. On top of the bombardment of information we absorb through these mediums from our friends and followings, they also contain advertisements, and a host of "this is how you should live your life" announcements continually. We've started viewing this as genuine life now.

Someone else provides the effort in producing or cooking our food for us, so we no longer grow (or appreciate) our own harvested crops. Someone makes our clothes for us. We're constantly entertained and distracted by a barrage of television shows and movies, which often include violent, unspeakable content. We pretend we're someone or somewhere else to essentially escape the world we're living in now.

Our newfound obsession with technology and digital social outlets has a basic premise to it in our need to fit in. By conversing via the Internet, we take away a lot of the fear of NOT fitting in. We can think carefully about our responses, craft posts and personas that match what we would deem as "fitting" for our online social circles. We take much of the risk of "real-time" relationships out of the equation. There is, of course, still destructive interactions such as cyber bullying. But even that has a person hiding behind a computer screen, escaping reality, taunting or degrading people from the comfort of their recliner. And as the victim being bullied, we often don't realize we have the power to simply turn the computer or phone off.

In real life, people may find out we're not perfect, or don't live the life that we portray to others online. Online, we can easily put on masks and avoid rejection much easier. It makes life much easier. Less work and less stress. Right? Not exactly.

Our need to grow and be socially active animals is an integral part of being human. As painful as it may be, we need the experience of rejection, the ability to laugh at ourselves, and the simple act of physical human interaction. What we're missing when communicating through the Internet, text messages, or phone calls is a pat on the arm, a handshake, a hug, or being able to empathize fully with someone by simply looking them in the eyes. We miss what someone's true intention and personality is when we remotely converse with one another. In the advent of smart phones, we've now taken things even a step further by making the use of the devices in the company of another's presence acceptable. It's actually okay to ignore people sitting in front of us in order to check our phones. It's acceptable to stare blindly at a screen that offers shallow entertainment at best, when someone of value is sitting right across the table from us.

Yet, we think we're progressing. One of the biggest challenges to becoming human again is to walk away from the technology from time to time. To wean ourselves from the need to incessantly check for updates, thinking we may be missing out on something. We need to shut them off, and deal with people face to face sometimes. For us, in modern times, this is a huge step forward, not backwards.

How many of us go to bed staring at our phones? Or check it immediately upon awakening? We have conditioned ourselves to be constantly plugged in. And what do we have to show for the benefit? Well, let's see... increased anxiety, depression, insomnia, and general decreased mental well-being. As a race, we've never been so inundated with information and attention-grabbing media. It's hardly fair to really call this progress, isn't it? I mean, is the way we've evolved technologically considered beneficial?

The need for comfort, as discussed earlier, is indeed the root cause of most of our modern maladies. I would go out on a limb to say that our obsession with avoiding discomfort and the lack of confrontations in our lives leads to obesity, depression, anxiety, loneliness, stress, and low self-worth. All of the things we shy away from or shun are exactly what we're getting. We're so busy hiding behind computer screens, overprotective parents, food, and shopping, that we forget the basics. We forget the character-building bumps we need to take and the strains of life we need to work through in order to become better people.

In short, we all need to go through some discomfort in life in order to be more compassionate, empathetic humans. It's as simple as that. We need to know, in many ways, what it feels like to wear that shoe (to step into the shoes of others and walk a mile in them). We need some gut-wrenching lows of life to learn important lessons and move on. We need to seek our limits and go beyond them. These important events in our lives make us who we are. Looking at them in the correct light, those events give us love, they give us wisdom, and they give us power. Resilience and grit are quickly disappearing from the average human, simply because we don't have to work so hard to obtain anything anymore.

A book, written by Jia Jiang, entitled Rejection Proof, deals with the feelings of discomfort when it comes to handling rejection. The premise of the book was an experiment the author undertook to help alleviate his horrible fear of rejection. He forced himself to go through a series of silly challenges meant to elicit a "no" or a rejection from strangers to his odd requests. He wanted to help himself build a resistance to the negative connotations he put upon himself when he was rejected. To his surprise, many of his requests (and there were some really off-the-wall ones) were actually accepted. People surprisingly said yes to many of them. This led him to realize, that with a good set of facts (a good argument), we can ask for and accomplish more than we think. Again, to his surprise, many of the requests challenged the people he was asking, giving them a sense of accomplishment with him in completing the request. In one request, he knocked on a random door of a homeowner in Austin, TX, dressed in full soccer garb, ball and all, and asked if he could play soccer in his backyard while the man took his picture. The author told the man it was for a project. "Sure," he said. Another request involved a Krispy Kreme donut shop and asking to have a special donut made, but in the shape of the connected Olympic rings (it was during the Olympics at the time). The lady thought about it and gladly obliged, taking on the "cool" challenge to get it done. She loved it. She loved the feeling of helping someone with his goals. Wouldn't you, too?

He was also rejected quite a bit, and the first few rejections hurt. They hurt his ego, and damaged his pride. He didn't give up, though, and those rejections, mixed with some surprising "yes" responses from the people he asked, made him stronger. The rejections didn't hurt so much, and he found himself gaining resilience in dealing with people and, more importantly, himself.

The moral of the story here is going beyond our comfort zones and what we can discover if we face our fear, become uncomfortable, and do things despite it.

This getting dirty approach to life helps us to regain our bearings and perspective on what's important and what isn't.

Of all the concepts in this book, this is one of the most important. Our natural instinct for comfort is actually hindering us. The pleasure points in our brains are screaming for more, and technology and processed food companies keep happily profiting from that demand by supplying our addictions.

By putting the brakes on what we want in the moment and delaying our instant gratification, we'll find our humanity increasing again. Our needs for material and creature comforts are leading us toward a lonelier, fatter, self-absorbed, and mindless existence. That doesn't sound like fun, does it? Taking away our comfort to be happier is an odd concept to grasp, but it really works. Like so many other things, our lives lack depth when there's no contrast.

Think about this for a minute. How would you know what true happiness is if you've never been sad or angry? All of these emotions have a reason and a purpose (granted, we inflame and exaggerate many of these as well). What a boring life it would be to simply feel one emotion, even if that emotion were positive.

Do you know what some of the best parts of a long hike are for me? No, it isn't necessarily the challenge, or even the view at the top. It's changing my socks back at the car when it's over. The gratitude I feel for the finished accomplishment is magnified, after miles and miles of rough, muddy terrain is the simple pleasure of putting fresh socks on.

So what helps us to move forward in facing our fears and stretching our comfort zones? Discipline, grit, determination, and resilience. That's it. I know a lot of books and self-help gurus will have some sort of new age plan to help you through that, but the answer is that simple. It's time-tested, proven, and effective. That's the time-tested formula for any successful endeavor in changing yourself.

Having a need and end goal to push us forward, and a drive to be better people can help us push through the boundaries that hold us back, and, in this case, if we're talking about our comfort zones, that's a lot. That's an enormous step. More like a leap of faith, actually. And that's why this tenacity is so important. Without that grit and without the end goal in sight, we'll prefer to just settle into our comfort zones again, and let life slip by.

Being an avid mountain climber, when people voice their concern over the potential dangers of that hobby, I often reply that I would rather die on a mountain than on a couch. I'm being dramatic, but the sentiment is still true. I really would rather have had the best learning experience I could possibly muster as a human on this planet, and have helped as many people and living beings as possible. I can't do that sitting on a couch.

It's been said that in an age of entitlement, we all act accordingly. A lot of what I'm presenting is hopefully eye opening. I say that, because I don't think many of us know life any differently than we do now, especially in developed countries. Many of us are going so against the grain of our instincts that we're confused and tired. Our egos crave the attention and prominence. We're offered the false promise of happiness when we acquire more, and more. As early humans, we were able to survive with a cave, furs, a spear, bowl, and spoon as our only possessions. As we've evolved, we've been led to believe that we need a large house full of essentially aesthetically pleasing junk. It's also been said that we were not created to simply be born, pay bills, then die. I fully agree with that sentiment.

We need to realize is how incredibly motivating pain is. Along with the contrasts we spoke about earlier (knowing true happiness after knowing pain), we need pain to elevate us as better humans. One of the worst lessons a parent can teach their child is to avoid pain at all costs. It's tough for parents to allow their children to make mistakes, and fall on their faces. It's a difficult process to see your child get rejected, called names, shunned, or emotionally hurt in any way. But it's necessary. I don't mean a lingering, emotionally abusive situation. There's no tolerance for that, but kids are going to call each other names. In boosting their own egos, kids will attempt to make themselves feel better, or even gain popularity, by lowering the self-worth of another for their own benefit.

It's always easy to say, after the road has smoothed out in your life a bit, and not quite as easy to believe when you're going through it, but thank goodness for all of it. I'm grateful for the bumps, the bruises, and the scrapes I've encountered in life. I'm also grateful for the happy times, friendships, and shining moments I've been blessed to experience. Actually, all of it has been an incredible blessing, because it's all a learning experience.

The trials and tribulations in life are what give it depth. They're what living really is, and isn't that what being human is all about? In the next chapter, we'll talk about the need to not only make but also embrace mistakes and encourage our failings. Doesn't that sound exciting? After reading this chapter, I hope you would think so!

Learning to Be Human Again

Embracing Mistakes, Encouraging Failures

One of the most important lessons in my life was this: we are not our mistakes. Pretty simple, right? Just like a lot of ideas contained in this book, though, it was (and sometimes still is) an incredibly hard lesson to learn. It's a truth I think you need to experience in order to realize it. So what do I mean by that? Well, you can make a sandwich. Does that mean you're a sandwich? Do you become the sandwich? It's the same easy concept with mistakes and failures. We can make (and should make) mistakes, but we're not the mistake we make.

Think of making a mistake as an event that's separate from who you are, like going to the circus, or getting gas for your automobile. It's something you do, it passes, and you move on. In the case of mistakes, it's important to take the time to reflect and learn the lessons from them so you don't make the same mistake, and move on. Again, it sounds simple, but it's much harder to practice.

We miss so many opportunities to grow, to better ourselves, and to better others because we're simply afraid to look stupid or silly. The most successful people out there are the ones who weren't afraid to try something new, and, more importantly, they weren't afraid to fail. They used their failures as stepping stones to lift themselves up to the next level to where they needed or wanted to be. They then repeated themselves, made mistakes, got better, and continued the upward spiral. Part of the joy of being human is that we can build upon our mistakes, we can effectively reason what we did right or wrong, and we can learn.

Can we learn the mistakes of others as well? Oh, yes! Very much so. I personally think there's still a value to making your own mistakes, but there are times we need to look to the example of others to help guide us along.

In the last chapter, I talked a lot about the need to be uncomfortable and the benefits to growing and forcing yourself out of your comfort zone. Making mistakes is one of the biggest hurdles when it comes to your comfort zone. Along with the status symbols, people are falsely striving for (the big house, perfect body, flashy car, etc.), not wanting to look dumb or foolish is near the top of the list.

I've known people who would rather jump out of an airplane skydiving than sing karaoke, speak in front of a small group of people, or dance at a wedding. They would choose a death-defying act, rather than the potential consequence of looking like a fool.

Having the ability to make fun of ourselves a bit and to stop taking ourselves so seriously is freeing. Once you don't care how people view you, many of those feelings of guilt, shame, low self-worth, and looking foolish disappear. Please learn the lesson that making honest mistakes and looking foolish sometimes is a necessary step in becoming a better human.

Another enormous reason we cringe at the thought of

making a mistake or going out on a limb is that we're actually afraid of success. Let me repeat that. Many of us are afraid to succeed. We're scared to death we may succeed in our endeavor. We may do well in what we reached out to accomplish. Why is this so scary for many of us? Well, there are a couple of different reasons we may fear and avoid success. The top reason is that we probably don't think we deserve it. We think, with our frail ego in charge, that we haven't earned the right or deserve the fruits of our direct efforts. Another reason we fear success is that it begs the question: what's next? Many of us love the thrill of reaching a goal, of striving for something we don't have or can't do at the moment. What happens when we finally reach that goal? The thrill of planning and executing is done, so we think. Then what do we do to top that? That part is our ego, of course, setting us up for the "If you accomplished this, the next accomplishment must be bigger" lie. I call baloney on that one. Any goal that helps you grow is a good one, and they all don't have to be monumental. To some people, one of your small goals is a monumental one to them.

Let's also be clear about my definition of success here. I mean accomplishing a goal at hand. It could mean anything from finishing a crossword puzzle to running for president. Whatever you've set your sights on to make you a more productive human being.

In seeking to accomplish our goals, our biggest fear is often failure. This holds true, especially for people with a perfectionist mentality. For perfectionists, life can be difficult. They not only raise the standards of their own actions to an unrealistic place but also often expect the same from those around them constantly. Perfectionists have a hard time resisting the urge to correct others, even for insignificant errors, such as incorrectly pronouncing a word, or not doing things according to what they may think is the right way. Perfectionists are aiming for a level of life that's simply unachievable, and mistakes are not part of that plan at all.

Perfectionists or not, we have to give ourselves the freedom and bigger picture knowledge to fail. Failure is a good, productive tool that helps us move forward, not backward. Picture a staircase with your end goal in mind. Many of the steps leading to the accomplishment of that goal are mistakes, not just successes. Don't be afraid to continue taking steps up to get to where you need to be. By avoiding those steps, you become stuck or simply turn around and walk back down the staircase, dejected.

To close the chapter, here are some simple truths that may help to free you from some of the burdens of making a mistake: No one is perfect. Nobody. There will be times you'll look foolish making a mistake. Guaranteed. Mistakes and failures are the building blocks for you to move forward and grow as a human, and a necessary tool in accomplishing your goals. The more mistakes you make and learn from, the easier it gets to grow. The more you grow, the better you feel, and the better equipped you are to help and effectively deal with others and yourself.

Learning to Be Human Again

Priorities and Values

The word character is one that's not frequently used in this day and age. I never want to sound like an old, cynical man shaking his fist talking about "when I was a kid…" but, in this case, some of that might seep through as we start to examine some values and priorities, and we start to ask ourselves "which of those are mine?" Let's talk about what our values and priorities are. Both are building blocks that help to make up our character and, to some degree, our reputation.

Values, which are often referred to as principles, virtues or morals (used frequently within religions), are set guidelines we put upon ourselves to help guide our actions not only in relation to ourselves but also in regard to society in general. They're building blocks that help us become who we are, or in some cases, who we want to be. Our reputation, or how others think of us, is directly linked to these. For much of this book, I've talked about not caring what others think about you, or it may seem that way. The truth is that, sometimes, it really does matter how people perceive us. Here are some examples of that: being prompt, generous, fair, kind, patient, and polite are often associated with "good" values or virtues, and there's a lot of truth behind this. They say a lot about who you are. Most of these values have to do with positively or negatively affecting others, which is why they're so important. When you run late, you're taking advantage of another person's valuable time. Having a good reputation for being prompt is a service you're doing to others in the long run. See the correlation?

Have you ever stopped to determine what your values and principles are? Are you striving to become a better person? Like whom? Pick a mentor who exhibits what you would like to be, and how you would like to be perceived as. What are their traits? Their values?

EXERCISE:

Choose someone you admire, and write down what you think their greatest values are. How would you describe their reputation? My personal values are generosity, humility, fairness, compassion, and tolerance.

In the list below, see if any of these are what you live by, or what you think a mentor would live by. Are there any you may have never seen? I personally think everyone should have a code by which they live, and that they should have some sort of a guiding list of principles they adhere to, no matter what. The list is far from complete, so if there are any not listed, feel free to include those in your list.

- **Authenticity**
- **Achievement**
- **Adventure**

- **Authority**
- **Autonomy**
- **Balance**
- **Beauty**
- **Boldness**
- **Compassion**
- **Challenge**
- **Citizenship**
- **Community**
- **Competency**
- **Contribution**
- **Creativity**
- **Curiosity**
- **Determination**
- **Fairness**
- **Faith**
- **Fame**
- **Friendships**
- **Fun**
- **Generosity**
- **Growth**
- **Happiness**
- **Honesty**
- **Humility**
- **Humor**
- **Influence**
- **Inner Harmony**
- **Justice**
- **Kindness**
- **Knowledge**
- **Leadership**
- **Learning**

- Love
- Loyalty
- Meaningful Work
- Openness
- Optimism
- Peace
- Pleasure
- Poise
- Popularity
- Recognition
- Religion
- Reputation
- Respect
- Responsibility
- Security
- Self-Respect
- Service
- Spirituality
- Stability
- Success
- Status
- Trustworthiness
- Wealth
- Wisdom

Now that we've chosen some principles and values, let's work on choosing our priorities. When we list our priorities, they're a little different than values or virtues (although, we can certainly prioritize our values). In choosing priorities, we're essentially asking ourselves, "What's most important?" Asking ourselves may be a stretch, because our actions are louder than our words in this case. Do you say your family is a priority over your cell phone? Television? Work? Really? Think about that for a moment. Is it really? That answer may surprise you.

Tomorrow, make a detailed list of where you spend your time. Take a notepad and jot down the times spent on whatever activities you did. At the end of the day, or the next morning, make an assessment. Are these activities good for you? For everyone around you? Do they help you to grow, or educate you? Help to push you out of your comfort zone a bit? After some meditation on where you spend your time and energies, make a new priority list. This time, think about where you should be spending this valuable time. Hiking with your family? Visiting the museum with a friend? Visiting a loved one and having a conversation with them with your phone off or, better yet, in the car or back at home? Can you volunteer somewhere? Bake something for someone? Use your talents to help someone who may need them, such as teaching folks in a nursing home how to use a computer, or playing songs for them if you play guitar. Again, strictly my opinion, but don't you think these are better ways to make things in your life priorities? Make a list of all of these things you can choose to do instead of casually strolling through life. I'm not saying that TV, or browsing the Internet are bad. We all need valuable downtime, and I enjoy

spending a little time on Facebook or watching a good documentary sometimes. You may have even found this book that way. These are healthy, normal activities. But the amount of time and priority we put toward them can make them unhealthy activities.

Finally, look at the list of values you wrote down, and compare them to the list of priorities you listed. Do they serve each other well? Chances are they do. If they don't, then you may need to tweak either of them a bit in order for them to align with each other.

What priorities are most important to you is a question you can only answer yourself, and, as I presented it in the last exercise, you can say what your priorities are, but your actions will truly define what they are more than a list ever will.

Can't We All Just Get Along? (Communication)

In an age of technology when directly communicating with our fellow human beings has never been easier, we've forgotten some important aspects of that connection. We may be able to physically speak to each other easier, but we've never been taught how to properly communicate. We know what we're thinking, and we know what we want to try and convey to another person, we just can't get the words or actions right to match with that feeling.

Wars have been fought, families have been ruined by divorces, and people have stopped speaking to each other for lifetimes all because we didn't know how to properly communicate with one another. Can you imagine the amount of suffering we could have saved, both with others and with ourselves, if we just could have communicated properly with each other? In this chapter, I'm going to present a few pointers to help you do just that. Communication isn't all that hard if you can find a middle ground that not only benefits both of you but also can present the facts without accusation or keeping the conversation one-sided.

So with all of this miscommunication going on, how do we communicate effectively?

There's no exact answer to that question, but it's not as difficult as you think. Much of this book has been devoted to many of the key elements required to pull off an easy communication session between people, believe it or not.

As we've spoken about earlier, perception has much to do with our success in bridging the gap in communicating. Remember the farmer and the jack story from earlier? Once we stop ruminating and stick to the facts at hand, we can make a far better assessment of what someone else may, in fact, be thinking or, more importantly, what their motives are. Motives behind someone's words or actions are important to flush out because we often misinterpret them as being hurtful or with ill intent behind them. In most cases, I don't think malice is behind someone's thoughts or actions. There's another reason, but we just interpret incorrectly.

Avoid sarcasm in conversations. You may know that you're joking, but the other person may not. You may be perceived as arrogant or flippant. In successful communication, helping the other person feel safe keeps dialog open and free flowing, and that's what you want. You want the conversation to stay meaningful and on point. When I say on point, I mean there needs to be a final outcome of the conversation that you want to happen or a conclusion you need to come to. Stay away from embarrassing or belittling whomever you're talking to. And keep an open mind; don't always assume you're right. After all the facts from both sides of the conversation are laid out to look at, you may find you are, in fact, the one who may need to change their attitude, perspective, or actions.

You never want to approach a conversation, especially a heavy one or a confrontation, with malice or hate. As we've discussed earlier, separate a person's actions or behavior from the person. You may be disappointed or hurt by their actions, but don't take it out on the other person. Avoid trying to get back at them, or trying to unnecessarily punish them.

As an example, let's say a coworker is playing their music too loud in the next cubicle at the office. Your main objective in a conversation like this is basically that they turn the music down or shut it off. That's your goal, the endpoint you need to address.

Instead of letting it build up and waiting too long to address, approach it early (again, remember the farmer and the jack story). Ruminating on why they may decide to play music that loud will only conjure up a number of false stories and representations of why they're doing it, to begin with. In approaching your coworker, be calm, polite, and direct. Gather up your facts before heading into the meeting, and remember that the ruminating stories are not facts. Your loss of concentration and productivity at work are facts. "I bet they're doing it because the boss likes them better, and they think they can get away with it" isn't a fact.

Remember to keep your main goal in mind, and be cautious not to steer away from it. Make sure the conversation is relevant to the subject at hand, and keep an open mind. State what you're looking for in having this conversation as accurately as possible, and any conclusions you may have, based on the facts at hand. "Fred, you may not be aware of this, but the volume of the music you play has been affecting my work performance here. I'm having trouble concentrating, and my productivity is suffering for it. Is it possible to come up with a solution that may benefit both of us?"

State your facts clearly and nicely, and you may find Fred didn't realize that he was bothering you. He may work much better with music playing, and he assumed everyone else does as well.

Again, perspective has much to do with a successful conversation, so keep an open, empathetic mind. Asking questions to gain perspective from the other person can also be an important tool in flushing out what they may be thinking, or behaving the way they are. Questions also are an easy way to eliminate false assumptions you may have from another person as well.

For example, your friend Jane has been avoiding you lately, and you may feel you've done something to initiate her colder nature towards you. You may ask questions like; "Jane, I've noticed we don't seem to connect as well as we used to, I feel like there's a wall being built between us now. Have I done something I'm unaware of to cause this?" or "Jane, I feel I've done something wrong and don't know what that might be. Our friendship is too important to let something like this slide, and I'd like to talk about it. Is now a good time?"

You may, in fact, find out that you did something that, in Jane's perspective, offended or hurt her. You could very well find out that Jane is having marital or work-related problems that she's having a hard time dealing with, and her cool nature has nothing to do with you at all.

Your goal is to always see things from the other side (keeping an open mind), gathering and sticking to facts, paying attention to what is being said (verbally and nonverbally) by the other person, and being careful in what you say in return. Come up with a solution or conclusion you would like to see from the conversation and keep a steady, open dialog by making each other feel safe and working together.

Effective communication is a very important and relevant part of the human experience, and we should treat it with respect. The benefits of communicating well are important factors in where you work, the relationships you have, and the ability to help others.

Learning to Be Human Again

Compassion, Empathy, and Forgiveness

Another of the greatest needs we all have in life is the need to be wanted, to be recognized, appreciated, and simply loved. Love can have many connotations and definitions to it, but, ultimately, it comes down to providing care, positive attention, empathy, and kindness toward our fellow human beings. Many of the world's problems are simply based on the selfishness of others, people only taking care of themselves. There's nothing wrong with that to a certain degree, and it's very healthy to look after yourself, but not always at the unnecessary expense of someone else. Unless we can live empathetically, we could very well be causing more harm than good. Empathy is the ability to understand and share the feelings of another.

There's a Buddhist saying that says the ultimate show of compassion and empathy is when you see a man beating an innocent dog, and you feel pity for the man.

That saying may have elicited some strong feelings in you against the man, but whether right or wrong, compassion, based on empathy, would have us feel pity toward that man or perhaps his suffering, upbringing, or maybe the extreme sadness or anger he's had in his life. Empathy isn't always an easy direction to head in. It's not easy for many of us to genuinely put ourselves in the shoes of another. But that's what's at the heart of compassion. Some of the most respected and loved leaders of our time based their morals on compassion. Martin Luther King, Gandhi, and even Abraham Lincoln were men of compassion and empathy. They led with an empathetic style that won the hearts of millions, nonviolently and peacefully. They knew that in every heart was the desire to both feel and outwardly convey love, and that was the overall plan for their successes. They knew that desire was what we all had in common. It's difficult to sometimes love or feel compassion toward one another, especially if we've been hurt by someone. But we can't give up on loving.

We start to lose our capacity for compassion when we start to feel unloved. We also have a hard time feeling empathy for others if we don't feel compassion toward ourselves as well. If we have low self-worth, instead of taking criticism well or brushing off others' opinions of us, we get defensive. We tighten up, and our defense mechanisms kick in. We become angry, sarcastic, cynical, bitter, and just plain nasty. Remember our list of core values earlier? Are bitterness, anger, sarcasm, cynicism, or jealousy on that list? Do those characteristics make for a great person? No? I didn't think so, either. Why would you want to exhibit any of those characteristics for any reason? One reason may be because your ego was hurt, and you want to hurt the other person in retaliation. If they hurt you, it's okay to hurt them, right? Think on that for a moment. The minute anyone has caused you to lose your sense of yourself or the situation at hand, they've already won. You've surrendered, and you didn't even know it. That person, or, more accurately, your emotions, has conquered you.

The underlying theme here is that we all suffer. Some of us suffer more than others do needlessly because we function better in doing so. And because we allow ourselves to suffer, we expect others to automatically know what our suffering is, and cater to what we think we need. People don't want to hear the idea that we cause most of our own suffering, but it's a concept we should all take the time to look into. We've made most of the choices in our lives that have brought us to the places we are now. We've earned as much money as we wanted, married whom we wanted, lived where we want to live, and chosen the friends we hang out with. Beyond all of those choices, we also choose to suffer. We're the ones who ultimately choose our reactions to life itself around us day by day and minute by minute. We choose what we'll do when circumstances, in our opinion, are less than perfect such as when the dog craps on the rug, the car won't start, we burn our dinner, and a bill comes due we didn't expect. It's our choice to either embrace anger and chaos or peace. That concept is a life-changing, eye-opening one for some. Do we really have that much power? We really do.

The world and people who surround you aren't your enemies. You are your own worst enemy. You're the one who holds yourself back, who sets your ultimate limits, and who chooses your own reactions. You choose to get upset; people don't "make" you upset. That's simply a ridiculous notion. Just as we spoke about in an earlier chapter, your life will change so much if you're just able to hold onto the concept that you're in full control of your thoughts, reactions, and actions. They're all your choices. You're responsible for them.

Even knowing that we're able to control our reactions, it's often difficult to control our emotions. When someone dies, we grieve; when we're rejected or break up with someone, we hurt. These are the times when compassion can play a crucial role in helping our fellow human beings.

As part of the process for being more compassionate humans, we need to address forgiveness. The very act of forgiving another puts a very sour taste in some people's mouths. I'll let you in on a little secret about forgiveness you may not know, though. You don't forgive others for their sake; you forgive others for yourself. Granted, there are times when your forgiveness means a great deal to others, and that's an added blessing. You're making the world a better place by helping another and letting them forget their mistakes. BUT forgiveness is ultimately for yourself. Letting go of all those pent-up emotions and freeing yourself of that burden is worth it. Does that mean you forget what may have been done to you? No. Does that mean you'll let it happen again? Again, no. Forgiving others, and yes, sometimes it takes a little time, will, ultimately, stop the festering of old wounds and allow yourself to heal. It's taking the adult approach of regaining empathy toward your aggressor(s) and freeing yourself from the shame, guilt, and regret associated with non-forgiveness.

And the ultimate forgiveness? Forgiving yourself. This is one of the most important steps toward becoming human again.

Realize that you, in all your mistake-filled glory, are human too. And that's perfectly, and wonderfully okay.

Give yourself the permission to free yourself of that burden. Go on, I dare you.

Conclusion

Life is ultimately a fleeting experience. A short time span, in the grand scheme of things. Time and energy are valuable and precious commodities, more valuable than anything this world has to offer. We have the power to control what we do, and when we do it, don't squander that power.

Being human, at its core, is much more than catering to outside influences, societal pressures, and the belief structures we've been taught to hold as truth. I think being human ultimately lies in our ability to stay present with who we are, what we're experiencing, seeing, touching, and smelling in the moments they occur. It means embracing and accepting all of what life has to offer us; pain, pleasure, mistakes, victories, lessons, and a full range of emotions associated with the whole adventure of being a living, breathing human animal.

Ultimately, underneath the police uniform, tattoos, beard, makeup, clothing, and hairstyle, we're all human. We all have a common connection to each other and have the responsibility in choosing to live a life that can be free of the unnecessary pressures we put upon ourselves to be more than we need to be.

We are all wonderfully created, complex, and ultimately physically imperfect creatures. What a great joy it is knowing we are so far from that perfection, yet still existing so beautifully.

We all feel joy, we all suffer. Everyone cries, feels the need for love, has worries, and experiences sadness. Deep down I believe we all want the same things. We want to cast away the false, controlling, and unnecessary expectations and pressures that have been thrust upon us, and take back the genuine experience of what it feels like to be a human again. All of us have the power to change our thinking and to remove many of our fears, worry, and feelings of inadequacy. We are in charge of our lives, and when we accept that responsibility, it gives us the freedom to be who we really are.

If you enjoyed this book, please pass it on to a friend or a loved one so they may enjoy it as well.

If you also feel so inclined, please leave a review on Amazon. Reviews are crucial to an author for sales of their books. I would be forever grateful for this small favor.

Much love to you all!

Learning to Be Human Again

Printed in Great Britain
by Amazon